BOOBS

WHAT'S ALL THE FUSS ABOUT?

Praise for *Boobs*

'Boobs. All women have them. But do we ever really think about them? I mean REALLY? We have such a delicate, complex, emotional and sometimes fraught relationship with them. For many of us, our boobs form an integral part of our identity, yet we rarely consider the impact of them on our lives. This is the book we need to place our boobs firmly in the spotlight, to give them the credit (plus sometimes, the difficult feedback) they deserve as not just women's body parts, but as our partners in the feminine experience.'

Mel Schilling, author and relationship expert on *Married at First Sight* Australia and UK

'*Boobs* is literally my favourite kind of book, written by women about women and their appendages, with flat-out honesty, a huge splash of humour and well-researched historical facts. This book had me hooked by the time I read the name of the chapters. Can't think of another book like this ... ever.'

Alison Daddo, author of *Queen Menopause*

BOOBS

WHAT'S ALL THE FUSS ABOUT?

DR LISA PORTOLAN
AND AMANDA GOFF

echo
PUBLISHING

Echo Publishing
An imprint of Bonnier Books UK
6/69 Carlton Crescent
Summer Hill NSW 2130
www.echopublishing.com.au

Bonnier Books UK
HYLO, 5th Floor,
103–105 Bunhill Row
London EC1Y 8LZ
www.bonnierbooks.co.uk

Echo Publishing acknowledges the traditional custodians of Country throughout Australia. We recognise their continuing connection to land, sea and waters. We pay our respects to Elders past and present.

First published 2025

Printed and bound in Australia by Opus Group

Editor: Emma Driver
Page design and typesetting: transformer.com.au
Cover design and illustration: Nada Backovic

A catalogue entry for this book is available from the National Library of Australia

ISBN: 9781760689919 (paperback)
ISBN: 9781760689926 (ebook)

About the authors

Dr Lisa Portolan is the author of *Ten Ways to Find Love ... and How to Keep It* (Echo, 2025) and *Love, Intimacy and Online Dating: How a Global Pandemic Redefined Romantic Relationships* (Routledge, 2023) and has a PhD on digital intimacy from Western Sydney University. She is a frequent commentator on love, sex and intimacy and the intersection with digital technology, and has appeared on *The Project*, the *Today* show and *Insight.*

Amanda Goff is a journalist and best-selling author, formerly known as Samantha X. She was a successful journalist in London, where she is from, and in Sydney, before ditching her nine-to-five to become Samantha X, Australia's most famous escort, at the age of 38. She wrote two best-selling memoirs – *Hooked* (Penguin, 2014) and *Back on Top: Confessions of a High-Class Escort* (Hachette, 2017) – and retired as an escort at 49. Her latest book is *Misfit: The Unravelling of Samantha X* (Echo, 2025).

Contents

Boobs: An intro

Boobs. Breasts. Mammary glands. Boobies. Titties. Ta-tas. Juggernauts. Charlies.

For 38 years, I didn't give much thought to my boobs – or anyone else's, for that matter. It's not that I wasn't aware of them. They'd been there since I was about 13. But growing up in the '90s, I was surrounded by girls in low-slung jeans and spaghetti-strap tops, idolising the waifish physiques of Kate Moss and Keira Knightley – whose chests, like mine, were flat.

It suited me perfectly. By the time I was 18 and had ingested a heady mixture of popular culture, I was styling myself as a slender little waif and forcing my genetics to align with the aesthetic of the time.

I had relationships, flings and moments of intimacy, yet no one ever exclaimed, 'Wow, your boobs are tiny!' No one mentioned my chest at all. I always felt sexy and, in hindsight, it seems that others thought so too.

In the professional world, men looked me straight in the eye, not at my chest. On dates, they asked about my career, their attention fixed on my face. To me, men were just ... men. Like women but with dicks. Perhaps a bit clumsy or clueless, but nothing more dramatic than that.

My wardrobe reflected this indifference. I wore functional bras from Bonds, went braless when I felt like it, and occasionally indulged in something lacy. I never stood in front of the mirror lamenting my flat chest or wishing it were different.

In fact, I considered myself lucky. My mum had large breasts, as did some of my friends – both real and augmented – and they often complained about them. Backless tops weren't an option for them, low-cut dresses felt too risqué, and nakedness brought sagging into sharp focus. Their frustrations only reinforced my belief that I'd hit the jackpot. No sagging, no restrictions – just freedom.

Of course, I was aware of the broader realities of breasts. The struggles of breastfeeding. The shadow of breast cancer. The mantra 'check your breasts' was familiar. And I did, briefly, during my shower routine. But that was it. Breasts were just there, a footnote in my life.

Until I met Samantha X.

At the time, I was hosting a successful podcast about love, sex and intimacy. It was the pandemic, and we were all locked down. I was deep in my PhD on dating apps and intimacy, gaining a reputation as an 'expert' in the field. But one name kept cropping up in whispers and bold suggestions alike.

'You must interview Samantha X.'

I hadn't heard of her.

'She's a high-end escort,' people said. 'Absolutely gorgeous, a former journalist and a best-selling author. You have to talk to her.'

'Why?' I asked, curious but unconvinced.

'She has a unique perspective on love, sex and men,' they replied.

A staunch feminist, I was committed to my own view of men: hopeless, hapless and generally the lesser gender. But the name wouldn't stop coming up, so I gave in.

I reached out to her on Instagram, fully expecting no reply. She had a gazillion followers, an online lingerie-and-sex-toy shop and a larger-than-life persona. My message was simple:

Hi, my name is Lisa Portolan. I run a podcast on love and intimacy and am working on a PhD on dating apps. Everyone keeps saying, 'You must interview Samantha X,' so I'm reaching out to see if you'd like to join the program. Thanks!

To my surprise, she responded within the hour:

Yes, absolutely. What time suits you? I'm doing nothing in lockdown and would love the distraction. PS. Dating apps are rubbish, aren't they? I got blocked from Bumble! Please!

Her humour and irreverence won me over instantly.

I was nervous before the interview. I always am when speaking to sex workers – they've had so much sex! They're paid for it! They must be great at it! Male sex workers, in particular, like to boast, which can be downright unsettling.

But Amanda Goff (Samantha X was her stage persona, which she has since shed) put me at ease within moments. She was irreverent, authentic and wonderfully quirky. We hit it off immediately.

But Amanda also revealed something I'd overlooked my entire life: the power of boobs.

'They're a source of power,' she once said. 'You can get away with murder if you have big breasts.'

They're also a source of woe: 'He looked at my breasts and immediately asked if I could suck his cock.'

And they're a constant dilemma. Once you understand their power, you see the two camps women fall into. Small-breasted women: treated like equals, with meaningful conversations but often seen as 'one of the guys'. Big-breasted women: granted favours and attention, but often perceived as sexual objects and treated inappropriately.

There's no in-between.

Now, five years after we met, Amanda is one of my closest friends – my collaborator, my confidante and godmother to my baby.

About two years ago, after yet another 'boobs episode', it occurred to me that it was time to investigate boobs. We'd both attended a business meeting in which the other party (male, of course) leaned across the table during a perfectly business-like conversation and asked Amanda, 'Are your boobs real?' As though the question sat just fine among the other business-like minutiae.

How would I – a woman sans boobs, or with very small ones – investigate such a weighty topic? I had to consult the yin to my yang of boobs. That's right: Amanda.

But you might be wondering: *why* write a book on boobs?

Because they matter.

Breasts are more than just body parts. They are symbols imbued with meanings that go far beyond biology. They carry so much weight, both literally and figuratively. They've been a canvas upon which societies have projected their anxieties, desires and ideologies. By writing about breasts, we are not just writing about bodies. We are writing about the forces that shape our identities and our lives.

This book is a patchwork quilt of personal musings, historical reflections and political rants, stitched together in a way that defies any tidy narrative. And boobs, in all their glory and complexity, are the star of the show – not as mere objects of beauty or shame, but as deeply human parts of our bodies.

We don't have all the answers about boobs – hell, we're not even sure how *we* feel about them most of the time. But that's precisely the point. This book isn't about providing definitive conclusions or creating a neat little box around something that's vast, complex and deeply ingrained in our culture. It's about asking the questions, poking fun at the ridiculousness and embracing the messiness of it all.

In advance, we want to apologise if any terminology used in this book is perceived as incorrect or offensive. We are accepting women who embrace and celebrate diversity in all its forms. We fully understand that no matter how carefully we approach these topics, we may unintentionally offend someone. However, our goal here is not to 'other' anyone. 'Othering' means treating a person or a group of people as different, diminishing them, setting them aside – and we've all been othered enough in our lives. Instead, in this chaotic, unapologetic whirlwind of the countless experiences we've gathered about boobs, we come with open minds and hearts, eager to explore, discuss and engage, with respect and inclusion for all.

We're not here to judge, shame or claim that we've figured out the ultimate truth about breasts. Instead, we want to create a space for authentic conversations – a place where all the confusing, conflicting and downright absurd aspects of boobs can exist without apology. We share stories of others – people whose experiences with their breasts have shaped their identities in unexpected ways – and we throw in a little humour because, honestly, what better way to confront the chaos than with a good laugh?

At its core, this book is a reclaiming of boobs. Not as something to be fetishised, idealised or confined to one narrow narrative, but as real, beautiful, strange and wonderful parts of our bodies that deserve to be celebrated – in all their forms.

• • •

CHAPTER ONE

A reader's note on droopage

So, you're about to sit down with this book. It's a decent size – not so short that you'll breeze through it in an hour, but not so long you'll feel like you're attempting *War and Peace*. On average, this kind of book takes six to eight hours to read, depending on your pace. This could mean powering through in one epic session, spreading it out over a couple of weeks or leisurely tackling it over a month in our stressful, fast-paced world. But while you're immersed in the humour, historical discovery and witty observations in this narrative, something else might be drooping. Yes, we're talking about your breasts, and the not-often-discussed topic of breast ptosis – the technical term for sagging – and whether your reading habits are somehow contributing to it.

Let's set the scene. You're cosied up on the couch, book in hand. You might be reclining, slouching or sitting cross-legged. No matter the position, gravity is doing its thing. Breasts, unbothered by clever quips, are subject to their own quiet drama: sagging.

Breast ptosis occurs over time, influenced by factors

such as age, genetics, weight fluctuations, pregnancy, breastfeeding and – contrary to popular belief – just being human. While reading isn't necessarily a high-risk activity for breast ptosis (it's not like jogging braless, after all), if you're hunched over a book, you're inadvertently aiding gravity in its lifelong mission.

Let's break down the science*

*FYI we are not scientists, nor are we medical doctors or mathematicians. Our conclusions therefore are largely fictional.

Factor 1: Duration of reading. If it takes you six to eight hours to finish this book, that's a significant chunk of time spent stationary. Whether you read it all in one go or spread it out, your breasts are enduring the relentless pull of gravity for those hours. Over the course of one book, the change may be imperceptible. But over many books? Let's just say that for bibliophiles, the cost of literary escapism might include a slightly droopier décolletage. Worth the droopage, many would argue – including the authors of said book!

Factor 2: Posture. The classic reading slump – a hunched position with your neck craned and your shoulders rounded – is not doing your breasts any favours. Poor posture accelerates the stretching of Cooper's ligaments, those delicate bands of connective tissue that keep breasts perky. If you're lying on your back while reading, however, you might be defying gravity temporarily, which is great for your breasts but potentially terrible for your neck.

Factor 3: The bra dilemma. Are you reading braless? Letting the girls roam free while you dive into the literary world? If so, gravity's pull is unhindered. Wearing a supportive bra during long reading sessions can mitigate ptosis, though lounging in lace isn't exactly the pinnacle of comfort.

Factor 4: Emotional turmoil. Does this book involve heart-wrenching drama? Laughter? Fear? Yes, absolutely! Emotional responses can lead to chest heaving, which – while not scientifically proven to cause sagging – certainly doesn't help matters. A sob-worthy chapter might cause more quivering than a steady, emotionless read.

The sagging maths

Let's crunch some numbers. Research suggests that on average, breasts sag about 1–2 centimetres per decade due to aging and natural wear-and-tear on the skin and ligaments. That's roughly 0.1 to 0.2 millimetres per month. So, if it takes you one month to read a book – not including the time you spend sleeping – you're looking at a truly minuscule amount of sagging during that time, possibly 0.002 millimetres per hour of reading.

Even so, your breasts likely sag more while you sprint for the bus than during a literary binge. But hey, why let facts get in the way of our analysis?

Let's imagine three types of readers to illustrate this point.

1. The Speed Reader (6 hours). This reader tears through these 50,000 words in a single sitting, perhaps fuelled by caffeine and the sheer joy of reading such intriguing stuff. They're likely seated upright at a desk or slouched on the couch, with their breasts hanging out in whatever direction gravity decides. Over six hours, they experience approximately 0.012 millimetres of sag. That's about the width of a human hair – hardly catastrophic.

2. The Casual Reader (2 weeks). This reader fits in 30 minutes a day over a couple of weeks. Their breasts endure daily gravitational exposure during their sessions, but because they break it up, the impact is negligible. Over two weeks, they might experience 0.014 millimetres of sag, a smidge more than the speed reader.

3. The Leisurely Reader (1 month). This reader takes their sweet time, reading a chapter here, a few pages there. By the time they finish the book, they've clocked the same six to eight hours, but spread out over 30 days. Sagging? Still around 0.016 millimetres, though the prolonged exposure to gravity might add a psychological toll as they reflect on the unfairness of time.

Overall, we conclude, all this reading is worth the droop.

So go on! Allow the girls to roam free. Sit back, relax, enjoy the read and sink – indulge – in the sublime droop!

• • •

CHAPTER TWO

Let's be serious about breasts ...

... for a moment.

Breasts are not just physical features on our bodies. They are also political, cultural and social symbols that have been shaped and reshaped by mainstream Western culture. And that culture is dominated by the people who hold political and economic power, who control the media narratives and who set the trends. Those who dominate popular media have created ideals around our breasts and bodies that perpetuate narrow standards of femininity and beauty. This means that our breasts are often a battleground for debates about power, identity and autonomy.

To write about breasts is to write about the construction of feminine identities – that is, how societies define what it means to be a woman. Breasts have been used as symbols of fertility, motherhood and sensuality, often without paying attention to the lived experiences of women themselves. These cultural constructions are not static; they shift over time. So, by examining how breasts have been represented in media, art and literature, we can trace how ideas about gender and femininity have evolved.

Take, for instance, the way breasts have been portrayed in advertising. Advertisements of the early 20th century often reduced women to their physical attributes, using breasts to sell everything from cars to hamburgers. Yet, in recent years, there has been a pushback, with campaigns celebrating diverse body types and challenging traditional notions of beauty. Young women, old women and women of different sizes and proportions are featured and celebrated. This shift reflects broader cultural movements we have seen, such as the push for gender equality and bodily autonomy (a woman's right to make decisions about her own body without coercion), but it also highlights how deeply entrenched the commodification of breasts remains.

The commodification of breasts refers to the capitalist system we operate in – to commodify something is to make that thing 'buyable' or 'sellable', to wrap it into a system of trade. And, like most things, boobs have been commodified. This will likely be the moment when Amanda rolls her eyes, a result of my 'leftie' dialogue. Perhaps it's important to note here that we do hold opposite ideological views along the political spectrum, and yet we coexist harmoniously.

This political dimension of breasts cannot be overlooked. Breasts have been at the centre of debates about women's rights, and these debates often expose the contradictions in how society views women's bodies. Breasts are celebrated as objects of desire in popular culture, yet their natural functions – like feeding a baby –

can provoke outrage or discomfort in public spaces. There is a tension here between the personal and the political – between a woman's autonomy and society's control.

Culturally, breasts are laden with expectations and judgements, and their size, shape and appearance can dictate how a woman is perceived. In Western culture, larger breasts are often sexualised, while smaller breasts might be dismissed or deemed less 'feminine', but these cultural scripts vary across different societies and historical periods. For example, during the Renaissance, fuller figures, including larger breasts, were celebrated as symbols of wealth and fertility. In contrast, the flapper era of the 1920s idolised a more androgynous silhouette, and flattened chests reflected a rejection of traditional femininity.

So how are these ideals about breasts and bodies perpetuated, and who decides what they are? Mainstream media plays a significant role. Hollywood, for instance, has long told us what the 'ideal' female body should look like, and breasts often serve as a focal point. Think of the iconic bombshells of the mid-20th century – Marilyn Monroe, Jayne Mansfield – whose curvaceous figures epitomised femininity for a generation. These images of beauty were often crafted through a male gaze, prioritising men's desires over women's realities. Think of those impossible 22-inch waists, which needed to be 'trained' into shape. Even the idea of 'training' a body part into a particular shape reinforces the idea it was never supposed to be that size!

But breasts are also sites of resistance, and feminist

movements have sought to reclaim the narrative around women's bodies. Artists, writers and activists have used breasts as symbols of empowerment, creating spaces for women to define their own identities. The Free the Nipple campaign of the 2010s, for example, demanded the right for women to go topless in public spaces – because if men could flaunt their hairy pecs at the beach, why couldn't women do the same? It highlighted the hypocrisy of a society that glorifies sexualised images of women's breasts while censoring non-sexualised depictions. Bodily autonomy was at the forefront of Free the Nipple, and campaigners argued for women's right to exist without being objectified.

Writing about breasts is also a way to explore how different aspects of women's identities – race, class, sexuality – intersect. Women of colour, for instance, have often been hypersexualised in ways that differ from their white counterparts, reflecting broader patterns of racialised sexism. Think about women of colour and bums. When did the big bum become a fashion statement? When did women start getting Brazilian butt lifts? When did big bums migrate out of a sphere that was traditionally associated with hypersexualisation of women of colour and into a mainstream domain? The name 'Kardashian' comes to mind ... and alongside it, the commodification of physical 'assets', as already described. Queer and trans individuals face additional layers of complexity as they navigate the expectations of society that may not align with their own identities.

In writing this book, we aim to challenge the dominant

narratives around breasts and offer a more nuanced perspective. We want to explore the ways in which breasts have been constructed in our sociocultural identities and reconstructed over time, and how these constructions reflect broader cultural and political dynamics. We want to highlight the voices and experiences of women, particularly those who have been marginalised or overlooked in the mainstream. And we want to celebrate the diversity of the human experience, recognising that there is no single way to be a woman, and no single story that defines what breasts mean.

Women are deeply aware of how breasts are both intensely personal and profoundly public. They are part of our bodies, yet they are often treated as public property, subject to scrutiny and judgement. From an early age, girls are taught there are rules associated with breasts and those rules can be contradictory. *Boys can have their nipples out. But not girls – it's indecent! Cover up! But not too much! Put a bra on – don't just let the girls dangle about! They're yours – but they're ours to comment upon!* Do you know any other body party which is subject to this level of public scrutiny? This paradox is at the heart of why we write about breasts.

It is an attempt to reclaim them – not as symbols imposed by others, but as aspects of identity that we define for ourselves. As women, we have a stake in defining what they mean – for ourselves, for each other, and for the world.

• • •

CHAPTER THREE

Grow some fucking tits!

Amanda

The pub was packed. Sweaty men were standing around in groups, cheering for some boxing match, downing beers and laughing loudly over the large TV screens while groups of screeching women stood in circles, clutching their warm sav blancs and trying to be noticed. One of those young women was me, standing awkwardly with my new friend – a very beautiful model called Charlie. She was capturing the admiring glances of men, who raised their eyes up to look at her glide past, only to quickly glue them again to the TV. Nothing comes between Australian men and their sport, not even a beautiful woman.

The year was 2000, and it was a balmy summer's evening at a pub in Sydney's eastern suburbs. I was 26 years old, having just arrived in Australia fresh off the boat from my hometown of London. I'd agreed to a two-year visa and a job at a celebrity magazine and off I went, not knowing a single soul. I just knew I wanted to be far, far away from the packed tubes – little incubators of anxiety for me – and the looming grey clouds all day, every day.

I had been a journalist in London on the tabloids and was now a journalist in the much calmer (and slightly less exciting) media in Australia. 'You can forget your career if you move to Sydney,' a famous showbiz reporter snorted to me when I said I was leaving the big smoke to start a new sun-soaked life in Bondi Beach.

He was right, of course. While Sydney was beautiful, sunny and easy, the media was gentle – a much slower pace with no real celebrities to write about. (The decent ones moved to LA or London. Let's be honest – they knew Australia wasn't great for their careers either.)

But what Australia *was* good for was having a better work–life balance, and being fit and healthy, which in turn meant I was more body conscious. And that meant everyone else was too.

'What's it like being the UGLY friend?' A drunk male voice jolted me from my people watching.

Um, what? I turned around to face a sunburnt man in a bright-blue Hawaiian shirt, spit glistening off his cracked lips, staring at me and standing so close I could smell his sweat.

'I said: what's it like being the ugly friend?' he slurred,

his bloodshot eyes trying to focus. I hadn't realised that Charlie had just rebuffed him, turning her back on this drunken pig, which meant he was left standing there feeling like an idiot, humiliated and, in turn, pissed off.

'Oh fuck off,' I replied bravely, being the second woman (but probably not the last woman that night) to turn my back on him.

'*You* fuck off. And while you're at it, grow some fucking tits.'

I spun around again. *What did he say? Is he actually talking to me?*

'Yeah,' he said, realising he'd got a bite. 'You heard. Grow some FUCKING TITS.' And he staggered off to join his mates, who hadn't even noticed their loser mate had disappeared. Either that or they didn't care.

My face burned up, and I felt myself pulling up my top to cover my cleavage. *Grow some fucking tits?* Did I not have any tits? No one, I repeat, *no one* had ever said that to me before. God, that was really humiliating. Charlie asked if I was okay.

'I'm fine,' I said. 'I'm just your ugly friend.' And we both laughed – hers genuine, mine fake.

I was mortified.

Was I ugly? Is that how Australian men saw me? Some ugly, flat-chested English girl with zero sex appeal? I know standing next to a model in a pub full of men is never a good idea but I wasn't that bad. Or was I? Was this it? Was no man in the whole big sunburnt country of Australia going to find me remotely attractive because I had no tits?

I didn't even really know I had no tits. I hadn't really given much thought to my breasts or my mammary glands before. As long as they were healthy and cancer free, what else mattered? I'd battled – and survived – anorexia in my teens. It took years, but the older I got, the less I cared about being skinny. And anyone who understands that eating disorder knows it's not so much about being skinny, it's about control. Starving yourself is a sign of desperate unhappiness and a huge cry for help.

But now I was happy. I had chosen to leave what was making me unhappy behind and start a new life. I was enjoying Sydney, my new job and, importantly, my body.

Besides, as a whole, us London birds didn't really give a shit about our bodies. We were pub girls; roast dinners and Yorkshire pud girls; apple crumble and custard girls. We didn't walk around in bikinis or activewear. We wrapped our bodies up in layers and layers of warm clothing.

No one in my life had ever commented on my breasts before – not in London, not on summer holidays in France, not in my relationships, not in my friends' circle. People in the UK in the 1990s weren't that bothered about being a size eight, or having the perfect body (whatever that even meant). We were getting pissed in pubs on cold rainy days; we were rugged up in poloneck jumpers and big heavy coats most of the year. We liked humour and banter and meat pies. We looked at faces, not bodies.

Supermodel Kate Moss famously once said, 'Nothing tastes as good as skinny feels.' And suddenly it occurred to me and my girlfriends: wait, were we *supposed* to be skinny? 'Heroin chic' became all the rage and having no boobs was trendy anyway – not that me or my friends really cared then. We were in our twenties, getting pissed in pubs or getting off our faces to house music in clubs. We didn't care about the size of our breasts.

It wasn't until that balmy summer night in a sweaty pub in a Sydney beachside suburb, with that disgusting man in the cheap blue Hawaiian shirt, that I realised two things: one, I had no tits; and two, it seemed as if I would have to grow some if I was ever going to get an Australian boyfriend.

What was to come I will get to, dear reader, but something happened to me after that. A niggling feeling in the back of my mind was born and it didn't go away.

Grow some tits? I did that as well, mate, going under the knife about six times, each time getting bigger, and bigger, and bloody ginormous.

I grew some fucking tits. Some fucking massive ones.

And it's been one of the best – and worst – decisions of my life.

• • •

CHAPTER FOUR

Memory of breasts

What is your earliest memory of breasts? Were they your mother's? That primal warmth, the soft scent of her skin, the incomparable safety you felt nestled against her? The kind of safety that comes with unconditional love and a meal always at the ready? Or did your first brush with breasts arrive via the pixelated world of pop culture?

Perhaps it was the surreal, gravity-defying spectacle of Pamela Anderson running down a sun-drenched beach in *Baywatch*, her chest bouncing in slow motion like two helium balloons tethered to her torso, defying not just physics but reason. Or maybe it was a diva on the cover of *Harper's Bazaar* or *Marie Claire* with extraordinary breasts, which we coveted.

Breasts, it seems, have always been in the frame – whether in the soft glow of maternal affection or the bright lights of celebrity spectacle. But isn't it funny how something so essential to human survival (hello, milk!) also carries such a ridiculous amount of cultural baggage?

For some of us, breasts began as a vague, comforting blur – your mother's gentle heartbeat under your ear, her scent a mix of baby powder and something indefinably hers. They were a part of you, or at least part of your world, long before you ever had a clue they could be anything else. Safety. Warmth. Home.

And then, puberty hits, and suddenly breasts are ... everywhere. On TV. In movies. On magazine covers. Whispered about, ogled and compared. It's no longer about comfort or safety; now, breasts are a currency, a statement, a whole identity. A girl's transition into womanhood, it seems, is often marked not by her first period but by her first bra – and the endless, unspoken competition of who has what, how much and how soon.

Of course, pop culture only turns up the heat. Pamela Anderson's red swimsuit in *Baywatch* wasn't just iconic; it was practically a monument. Breasts in media are big (literally), bold and unapologetic. And for the rest of us mere mortals, they're both aspiration and albatross.

Media and society tend to suggest that women with big breasts collect babies and press them to their chests and babies seem perfectly happy to be there. They fall asleep on pillowy breasts, drooling peacefully ... or, if they're not sleeping peacefully on their mother's breast, society will tell you it's because they can smell the milk! They're distracted! Meanwhile, on an exposed rib cage, babies will struggle, their heads maniacally shifting from side to side. Contradiction, contradiction, contradiction.

But think about it – when was the last time a man gazed at his chest in the mirror and thought, *Wow, these pecs could really use some work before beach season*? Breasts, on the other hand, are a never-ending project: scrutinised, judged and debated, even by their owners. Too big? Too small? Too saggy? Too fake? It's exhausting, really.

So, what's your first memory of breasts? Is it the nurturing comfort of your mother's embrace? Or is it the impossible, sunlit perfection of pop culture's most celebrated chests? Maybe it's a bit of both. Either way, one thing's for sure: wherever breasts entered your story, they've probably stayed, one way or another.

And, in the end, maybe that's the real power of boobs. They're soft, they're strong, they're ridiculous – and they're unforgettable.

• • •

CHAPTER FIVE

Lunch with James

'If I were straight, I think I'd prefer women with fake boobs.'

It was a hot summer's afternoon in Paddington, and James and I had decided to treat ourselves to lunch at a quaint little Italian place on one of those leafy streets that screams 'I have disposable income and a Lululemon membership'. Naturally, we didn't fit in at all, which only made us love it more. The restaurant had the kind of vibe where the tables were just a little too small, the wine was just a little too pricey, and the clientele was just a little too Botoxed. But the spaghetti vongole? Worth every penny.

We were seated in the back, under a framed black-and-white photograph of a very brooding Sophia Loren holding a cigarette, as if daring us to feel bad about our carb consumption. Around us, the 'ladies who lunch' were in excellent form – pearls, Pilates arms (no tuckshop arms in sight!) and Prada loafers, daintily swirling forks through salads they clearly resented. James and I, on the other hand, were going full hedonist: spaghetti vongole for both, garlic bread we didn't need, and a bottle of white that had indulgence written all over it.

'So, how's the book going?' James asked, twirling his fork like a cat playing with yarn.

'Good,' I said, taking a sip of wine. 'I'm deep in the research around breasts.'

James nearly choked on his spaghetti. 'Of *course* you are.'

'No, I'm serious! They're fascinating – politically, culturally, everything. Breasts are like ... the Switzerland of the human body. Neutral, but somehow always involved in a conflict.'

James snorted. 'Neutral? Darling, they're the NATO of anatomy. Everyone's obsessed, everyone's got an opinion, and they're always at the centre of some ridiculous war.'

I grinned. 'Exactly. I've been writing about how they're celebrated and censored, worshipped and weaponised, all at the same time. Like, take the Free the Nipple movement. Women fight for the right to just exist without being policed, and men act like it's the end of civilisation. It's fascinating – and exhausting.'

James leaned back, considering this as he chewed. 'You know,' he said finally, 'if I were straight, I think I'd prefer women with fake boobs.'

I paused, fork halfway to my mouth. 'What?'

'You know,' he said, gesturing vaguely, 'they're just ... more bulbous. Like little round works of art. Very symmetrical. Pleasing to the eye.'

'James,' I said, setting my fork down, 'did you just say you'd prefer *fake boobs* because they're more *aesthetically pleasing*?'

He shrugged. 'If I were straight.'

'Why do you think that is?' I asked, narrowing my eyes. 'You're a gay man, and you don't even like boobs. So where is this opinion coming from?'

He pointed at me with his fork. 'Conditioning. It's all contemporary culture. Fake boobs are like the Birkin bag of body parts. You've been trained to want them, whether you like it or not.'

I laughed so loudly the Botox brigade turned to glare at me in unison. 'You're saying the beauty industrial complex is out here brainwashing us into liking tits that look like basketballs?'

'Exactly,' James said, unfazed. 'Think about it. Fake boobs are everywhere – billboards, movies, Instagram. They're the gold standard of unattainable perfection. It's like we're all living in a Michael Bay movie, where explosions and enhanced cleavage are the height of cultural achievement.'

I picked up my glass of wine and took a long sip. 'So, what you're saying is, the male gaze has essentially colonised women's chests.'

'Darling,' James said, leaning in conspiratorially, 'it's colonised everything. Boobs, butts, cheekbones, lips. If you let them, they'll try to colonise your elbows.'

'Free the elbow,' I muttered, and James howled with laughter.

As our conversation continued, the ladies who lunch continued their ritualistic performances around us. One of them was delicately picking at a single ravioli like it was a bomb she was trying to defuse. Another was laughing into her phone, not quite loud enough to be obnoxious, but just loud enough to let us all know she was laughing into a phone. They were all impossibly chic, and somehow all had hair that looked like it had been blow-dried by angels.

'You know,' James said, gesturing to them with his wine glass, 'I bet none of these women have eaten a carb in a decade. Meanwhile, here we are, devouring spaghetti vongole like it's our last meal.'

I raised my glass. 'To carbs and body autonomy.'

'To carbs and boobs,' James corrected, clinking his glass against mine. 'And to questioning the patriarchy while eating garlic bread.'

The garlic bread, by the way, was exceptional – warm, buttery and just garlicky enough to ruin any chance of social interaction for the rest of the day. Not that we cared. We were deep in the trenches of feminist theory and cultural critique, using breadsticks as metaphorical swords.

'Do you think that the obsession with fake boobs is tied to this weird fear of imperfection?' I asked, swirling my wine. 'Like, real boobs sag, they move, they're unpredictable. But fake boobs? They stay put. They're controllable.'

James nodded thoughtfully. 'Yes. It's the same reason people love Botox. It's all about control. Control over age, over gravity, over chaos. Fake boobs are like the Swiss watches of body modification – expensive, precise and always ticking in the right direction.'

I laughed. 'I'll leave it to you to compare boobs to luxury timepieces.'

'Well, I'm not wrong,' he said, finishing his pasta with a

dramatic flourish. 'And honestly, it's a bit sad, isn't it? Real boobs are like art – imperfect, unique and full of history. Fake boobs are ... NFTs.'

'Not NFTs!' I groaned, nearly choking on my wine.

'Yes, darling. Shiny, overvalued and utterly devoid of soul.'

At this point, the waitress arrived to clear our plates, and I could feel her silently judging us for how clean we'd left them. Not a single clam remained, not a trace of sauce. We were unapologetic gluttons, and we owned it.

'Dessert?' she asked, raising an eyebrow.

James looked at me. 'Tiramisu?'

'Obviously.'

When the tiramisu arrived, we dug in with gusto, our earlier conversation taking a brief hiatus as we focused on the layers of mascarpone and espresso-soaked sponge. Around us, the ladies who lunch were wrapping up, gathering their handbags and their judgements, leaving us alone in the restaurant's post-lunch lull.

'You know,' James said, licking his fork, 'this whole conversation has made me appreciate boobs more. Fake or real, they're kind of amazing. They feed babies, they make men stupid, and they're the only body part with a built-in cushion. Genius design.'

I shook my head, laughing. 'You're ridiculous.'

'And you love it,' he said, raising his glass for one final toast. 'To boobs, in all their forms. May they continue to confound, captivate and inspire us.'

'To boobs,' I agreed, clinking my glass against his. And

with that, we drained the last of our wine, finished our tiramisu and stepped out into the Paddington sunshine, feeling lighter, happier and just a little bit tipsy.

As we walked down the street, James turned to me. 'You know, if this conversation makes it into your book, I expect royalties.'

'Darling,' I said, looping my arm through his, 'you'll get a footnote at best. You're heavy on the metaphors today and it's giving me a headache.'

He pretended to be offended, but I could see the smile tugging at the corners of his mouth.

'PS. I'm joining the Ozempic crowd next week.'

'You're going on Ozempic?' I laughed. 'You've lost it – you don't have diabetes and you're not overweight!'

'Like I said – social conditioning. One could always be thinner – and as a gay man, I too have been colonised by the male gaze ... and, come to think of it, the female one too!'

'Oh piss off!' I chortled.

'No more spaghetti vongole for me.'

'This is truly a terrifying and distressing state of affairs,' I intoned.

'If you can't beat 'em, join 'em.'

• • •

CHAPTER SIX

Why do humans have boobs?

Humans are the only mammals whose breasts stay puffed up like balloons once we hit puberty (you know, that awkward phase when we grow all sorts of things).

Yes, let that sink in. *We are the only mammals on the planet with permanent boobs.*

Why this happens, though, is still a mystery.

Scientists have a few quirky theories.

One theory suggests that breasts grew big because of a connection to fat storage and brain power. The body creates a hormone precursor (a pre-hormone, let's call it) called dehydroepiandrosterone, in fatty areas like the butt and breasts, and this may have helped our brains grow bigger over time. Who knew those curves were helping our minds evolve as far back as *Homo ergaster*, around 1.5 million years ago?

Then there's the handicap principle (say that ten times fast) proposed by plant biologist and evolutionary biologist (respectively) Avishag and Amotz Zahavi. This one says that big breasts are like a flashing neon sign saying, 'Look at me! I'm healthy and strong enough to carry these around!' Basically, it's like a fitness test for potential mates to see if they can keep up with the energy demands of supporting all that, well, *support*.

The famous zoologist Desmond Morris thought breasts were just like big squishy signals, just as a bigger, puffier backside had been (thanks, bipedalism). These sexy signals, along with other body parts, kept early human couples connected, even when they were doing separate chores and stuff. So, basically, bigger breasts = more bonding. (It's science, people!)

Another theory suggests that boobs got round because human babies have tiny jaws that don't stick out far enough to latch onto flatter chests without suffocating. Imagine that! A bigger chest meant babies could feed safely without getting a faceful of breast tissue.

And then there's anthropologist Ashley Montagu's take from 1965. He thinks breasts evolved because, as humans became upright walkers, babies couldn't cling onto their mothers' backs as easily (no more hairy monkey backs to hang on to!). So, as mothers began to carry their babies in front of them, big, mobile breasts made it easier for babies to find their food source and latch on. So, there you have it! Any of this make any sense to you?

• • •

CHAPTER SEVEN

The quest for Bridgerton Boobs

In the age of Netflix bingeing, nothing has captivated the collective imagination (and wardrobes) quite like *Bridgerton*. Beyond its scandalous plot twists, dashing dukes and faint-worthy declarations of love, there's one thing that stands out: the boobs. As we embarked on writing this book, we were consistently smashed in the face with articles about 'Bridgerton Boobs'. Written by women!

Yes, the boobs, you read it correctly: Bridgerton Boobs. Perfectly perched, improbably rounded and always showcased to full advantage in gowns that appear stitched by angels and reinforced by the gods. They're not just a fashion statement – they're a gravitational miracle. Watching these heroines sashay across the screen, I started to wonder: were women in Regency England just naturally blessed with superior décolletages, or was there some sorcery at play? Did they have a higher body mass index than modern women who are fixated with the gym, muscles and #stronggirl aesthetics? Was it the fashion that squeezed and positioned their breasts to appear like Bridgerton Boobs? Or was this, again, a poor representation of women and breasts of the time – a sexualisation of Regency England boobs, so to speak? And, if so, could I transform my own modern, sans augmentation breasts into Bridgerton Boobs?

In my research, I discovered that this quest for Bridgerton Boobs was not unique. The internet is awash with this concern.

And so, the quest begins – a personal odyssey to achieve the elusive Bridgerton Boob. Spoiler alert: it's a journey paved with corsets and confusion.

Attempt 1: The Corset Catastrophe

The first step to Bridgerton Boobs is, of course, the corset. Ah, the corset – the devil's undergarment, a medieval torture device, and yet the holy grail of boob boosting. Women in Regency England laced themselves into these contraptions daily, all in the name of societal expectations and chest elevation.

For the purposes of research, I decided to give it a go. Armed with a cheap corset from the internet (because nothing screams 'authentic Regency fashion' and 'modern slavery' like a suspiciously plastic-looking garment from an online mega-retailer), I embarked on my journey.

Five minutes in, I was sweating profusely, and the corset had a vendetta against my internal organs. 'This is fine,' I told myself, ignoring the ominous creaking noises as I yanked the laces tighter. Somewhere in the distance, I swear I heard a rib crack.

Finally, I stood before the mirror, triumphant. My

boobs were, indeed, hoisted. Elevated. Dare I say ... regal? But at what cost? Breathing was a distant memory and sitting down was no longer an option. Still, I felt closer to Bridgerton glory.

Attempt 2: The Bra Ballet

Not everyone is ready to commit to full corsetry (and, honestly, the hospital bills). Enter the modern equivalent: push-up bras. These marvels of engineering promise the same lifted, rounded effect without the organ compression.

I wandered into a lingerie store and was immediately confronted by a wall of bras with names like 'Extreme Lift', 'Double Up' and 'Mount Olympus'. Honestly, the feminist in me screamed bloody murder. The sales assistant assured me that these bras would transform my chest into the stuff of Regency dreams.

I left the store with a bra that felt like it had the padding of a couch cushion. When I put it on, my boobs were ... well, high. But they didn't quite have that Bridgerton oomph. They were perched. I had to face it: they lacked the volume required, push-up bra or no push-up bra.

Attempt 3: The DIY Disaster

After the Corset Catastrophe and the Bra Ballet, I turned to the time-honoured tradition of DIY solutions. Surely, with a little creativity and duct tape, I could achieve the perfect Bridgerton cleavage.

I found an online tutorial that promised 'Hollywood-level cleavage with just household items!' The method involved tape – lots of tape – and a deep-V-neck dress. I got to work, plastering my chest like an overenthusiastic crafter at a duct tape convention.

The result? A Frankenstein's monster of a cleavage. Sure, my boobs looked vaguely Bridgerton-esque, but they were also asymmetrical and slightly immobile. Plus, peeling off the tape was an experience I wouldn't wish on my worst enemy.

Attempt 4: The Regency Gown Revelation

By this point, I was ready to throw in the towel – or perhaps a lace handkerchief, in keeping with the Regency theme. But then I stumbled upon the key to Bridgerton Boobs: the gowns themselves.

The secret isn't just what's under the dress; it's the dress itself. Regency gowns are specifically designed to showcase cleavage. The empire waistline, the structured bodice, the strategically placed embroidery – it's all a masterclass in boob presentation.

I ordered a replica Regency gown (because of course I did) and slipped it on. Suddenly, there they were: Bridgerton Boobs in all their glory. No tape. No plastic-filled bras. No corset-induced asphyxiation. Just the right dress, doing all the heavy lifting.

Nope – I'm lying. Still not there. For anyone blessed with a flat chest, creating the perception of breasts and Bridgerton Boobs is virtually impossible. Perhaps a 'Regency Breast' filter might do the trick? Meta, TikTok – any thoughts?

• • •

CHAPTER EIGHT

So I grew some tits!

Amanda

My first boob job was in 2004. I *think*. I say 'I think' because I have an awful memory. It could be a sign of old age (50), some terrible disease that I don't know I have (or have forgotten I have) or the amount of damage I did to my brain cells partying (now almost seven years alcohol free, thank you very much).

But do you really care about the year? That's not the important bit. The important bit is what happened next.

Soon after that comment in the sweaty pub on the balmy night in Bondi, I met a man that I ended up having two kids with. We met walking our dogs on Bondi Beach. A quick hello in the mornings became dinner, then love. He didn't mention my breasts – ever. He was sporty and fit; I'd guess he was more a fan of Sporty Spice (Mel C) than the Big-Boobed One (Geri).

We had a nice life, living in a nice home, doing nice things. I was 29. *This is it for me,* I thought. *I'll have children with this man and that will be the next 25 years of my life sorted.* I had an enviable and sought-after job as a beauty director of high-end glossy magazines and was privy to the names and private numbers of the best surgeons in Australia, as well as to the best beauty treatments.

I suddenly became cocooned in the pink, fluffy world of beauty. I was offered trips, gifts and beauty treatments like I was a celebrity, all in exchange for nice write-ups in my shiny and influential magazines.

I was flown to London, business class, to interview a skincare scientist (who literally stormed out of the office when I asked if his 'miracle' skincare cream could really penetrate into our skin and make our wrinkles disappear as promised). Actually, looking back on it, he didn't actually answer my question, so I'll never know. (If you want to know the secrets of good skin, go to the end of my final chapter on page 228 and I'll tell you ... but don't tell anyone else.)

I interviewed fragrance experts, makeup artists, cosmetic surgeons and my favourite people – plastic surgeons. I knew about new treatments and procedures before anyone else did. An editor I'd once worked with on a weekly magazine joked to me that when she died, she wanted to come back as a beauty editor.

We both laughed, but it was true: I was living the fucking dream. I had a great job. I started wearing a lot of makeup and tried every beauty treatment under the sun. Half my week was taken up by facials, massages and beauty launches.

My friends were equally delighted, as I'd bring them bags and bags of goodies from the beauty cupboard. Their eyes would light up and they'd gasp excitedly as they tore open endless lipsticks and face creams. But if you're exposed to lipsticks day in, day out, it kind of loses its gloss (pun intended, although not planned; the gag was sheer luck).

I started to pay close attention to my body. It was hard not to. I wrote about faces and bodies all day. What's in, what's out. What's hot, what's not. What women want, what they don't want. What procedures they're having, what they're not having. Which body shapes are in, which are not. And what's on the rise in plastic surgery. And the answer, around 2004, was breast augmentation – the boob job.

Twenty years ago, women had boob jobs, but they weren't as common as they are now. Now it seems everyone bloody has them and no one bats an eyelid.

Breast augmentation is one of the most popular plastic surgery operations and it is reasonably simple to do. I know this because I interviewed one of Sydney's most renowned breast surgeons, Dr Steven Liew from Shape Clinic in Sydney. (A fantastic surgeon – highly recommend.) I can't remember the details of what we discussed but I do remember walking out of there thinking, *That's it. I'm getting a boob job.*

Speaking to Dr Liew, I realised that boob jobs were on the up, and that it wasn't a complex operation (usually). I would just go into the clinic, have a couple of consultations, decide what size to have and book a date. I wouldn't even need an overnight stay. It seemed ... easy?

I do remember Dr Liew and I discussing sizes. Being an A cup (or a small B), and a journalist, I didn't want to go *big* big. I didn't even think about going *big* big. I just wanted some boobs, for god's sake. Just some boobs. But how big (or small)? I had no idea.

'Do you want people to notice you on the beach for having big boobs? Or do you want a more natural look that fills out your clothes nicely and evens your body up?'

'Natural' sounded good. We decided on an implant of about 375cc (a large B or small C), positioned behind the muscle (more painful but more natural) and filled with silicone gel (the saline ones can burst and look too fake).

So I did it. I had my first boob job. I went under the knife for the sake of having bigger boobs.

So what can I tell you about it?

It was painful. It was *really* painful. My partner came to pick me up and went pale at the sight of two drains coming out of my chest and filling up a plastic see-through cup with my bright-red blood. I don't remember much, but I do remember the pain. I can best describe it as like having an elephant sitting on my chest. On the drive home, every stop and every speed bump felt like the elephant had decided to start jumping around. It was agony.

But who cares? I had boobs. I had beautiful, big, swollen boobs. They were big (hey – a big B, little C *was* big in my eyes back then), they were swollen (effect of surgery; unfortunately does not last), and they looked *fantastic* in bras and tops (after the 12 weeks of recovery wearing a daggy post-op bra).

During the next few weeks, I clearly remember going for a walk on the sand at Bondi Beach where I lived, and still live. I wore a tiny crop top and shorts. For the first time in my life, I noticed men looking at my chest. Each stare was a jolt of excitement, and ... validation?

I had boobs. I had boobs! I was now a woman with boobs. I was delighted and excited. I felt sexy, fit and in proportion as I walked faster and faster on the sand, my hips wiggling, sticking my new chest out and grinning ... until a man and his mate walked past me and I caught the tail end of his conversation to his friend. Words I still remember to this day.

'And see, mate? Look at that. Fake tits. Bondi is full of fake women like that.'

His mate turned to look at me and sniggered, and they walked away in male-bonding tut-tutting.

My face fell. *Wait, what?* Did I look stupid? Was I some kind of joke now that I had boobs? Did I look too fake, too big, too much? But ... but ... the looks, the grins, the sneaky side stares.

Had I got it completely wrong? And why did I bloody care so much?

I had a partner. I shouldn't have cared much about what men thought, about feeling sexy and desirable and wanted. But I did. I did care very much. I could go here into feelings of insecurity, needing validation from men because I didn't receive a mother's love as a child, blah blah, but this isn't one of my other books and you are not my psychologist (you can breathe a sigh of relief, believe me). It doesn't really matter why I needed male attention but there was something inside me that craved it. And I had thought the answer was getting big boobs.

But this was just the tip of the iceberg. My first boob job was just the beginning of a very long and complex journey.

My life was about to change in a huge way, a way I didn't even think was possible. I didn't realise I was about to turn my safe, conservative, middle-class world upside down, walk out of the relationship and my socially acceptable (yet often unethical) job in the media, and go on to become Australia's most high-profile escort, a best-selling author and the owner of the biggest boobs you can legally get in this country.

• • •

CHAPTER NINE

A perforated eardrum and Catriona Rowntree's breasts

It started with a mild cold that turned into a symphony of ailments. For weeks, I felt off-kilter: achy, tired and a little like a walking Petri dish. But life doesn't pause for illness, especially when you're juggling a PhD, a podcast and, for some inexplicable reason, a live interview on New Zealand television about dating apps and intimacy.

On the day of the interview, I wasn't exactly in peak condition. My throat was scratchy, my nose resembled a leaky tap, and my ears felt like they were stuffed with cotton balls soaked in regret. But the show must go on.

The studio was buzzing when I arrived, all bright lights and serious people with clipboards. I nodded politely, feigning health and enthusiasm. The topic of dating apps and intimacy is my wheelhouse, and I wasn't about to let a little thing like 'feeling like death' stop me from delivering hot takes about Bumble.

The interview started smoothly enough. I was mid-monologue about how dating apps have changed the way we approach love when it happened.

Snap. Crackle. Pop.

At first, I thought someone had crunched a particularly aggressive handful of Rice Bubbles nearby. But no. The noise wasn't external – it was inside my head. Specifically, in my right ear.

Then came the warm liquid. A trickle of something distinctly not normal started oozing out. I froze, mid-sentence, trying to maintain composure as my brain screamed, 'What the hell is that?!'

I powered through, keeping my face as neutral as possible. I couldn't tell if the camera operator was zooming in on my face, but I prayed he wasn't catching the moment the fluid from my eardrum decided to make its dramatic exit from my anatomy.

When the segment finally wrapped, I excused myself with as much dignity as a woman leaking ear fluid could muster. The cameraman, bless his oblivious heart, told me afterwards that he hadn't noticed a thing. 'You were great,' he said.

Great? I was now deaf in one ear, and the applause was ringing in my head like a cruel taunt.

I did what any sensible person would do: googled 'ear exploding' and promptly panicked. The internet, as always, was a mix of terrifying diagnoses and advice to drink water. Finally, I decided it was time for the professionals.

I took myself to the emergency department of my local hospital, where the waiting area was a mix of humanity in various states of disrepair. I checked in, sat down and stared at the television mounted high on the wall, which was playing daytime fluff. My ear throbbed like a disco beat.

Half an hour later, my partner arrived. He's the kind of guy who can make waiting rooms tolerable, cracking jokes and making snarky observations about the people around us. We laughed about the absurdity of my eardrum bursting on TV. We chatted about the interview, which he swore was excellent, despite the fact that I'd been one snap-crackle-pop away from an on-air meltdown.

Then it happened.

The segment on TV switched to Catriona Rowntree, Australia's beloved travel show host and perennial ray of sunshine, doing a piece on tropical destinations. She looked like a perfectly polished human embodiment of a Qantas ad. My partner's face lit up.

'Ah, Catriona Rowntree,' he said wistfully. 'She was my first crush.'

I glanced over, intrigued but wary. 'Really? Why her?'

He didn't miss a beat. 'Her boobs. They were huge.'

It took a second for his words to sink in. I stared down at my own chest – modest, functional and currently hidden under a sweatshirt that screamed 'I'm not well.' A tidal wave of inadequacy washed over me.

My eardrum just burst on national television, I thought, *and now I'm also deficient in the breast department?* Fantastic.

I tried to laugh it off, but inside I was seething. Who says that to their partner while they're literally *in an emergency room*? My mind spun with questions. Was he silently comparing my chest to Catriona's? Was I now competing with a woman who wasn't even aware of my existence?

Meanwhile, my earache pulsed with a vengeance, as if it

were mocking me. I cursed my partner. I cursed Catriona Rowntree. I cursed the entire male gender for its inability to filter commentary on women's anatomy.

My husband, of course, remained blissfully unaware of my internal meltdown, happily commenting on how good Catriona still looked.

Finally, my name was called. I trudged into the exam room, where a kindly doctor examined my ear with a gadget that looked like it belonged in a sci-fi movie.

'Yup,' he said after a moment. 'You've got a perforated eardrum. Looks like it burst recently.'

I nodded, feeling vindicated but also absurdly defeated. My eardrum had burst on live television, and now it was official.

'What caused it?' I asked.

'Could've been the pressure from an ear infection,' he explained. 'Or sometimes these things just happen.'

Just happen? Great. So, my ear had betrayed me without warning or reason.

He gave me a prescription for antibiotics and a pep talk about how eardrums usually heal on their own. I thanked him and walked back out to the waiting room, where my partner greeted me with a grin and zero awareness of the existential crisis I'd been stewing in.

• • •

CHAPTER TEN

'Imagine! Men wandering around with trousers featuring a little chipolata ...'

My friend and I were out one Saturday, indulging in what we like to call 'retail therapy for the soul', though it was mostly an excuse to complain about our lives while flicking through racks of overpriced clothing. The setting was the Broadway shopping centre, the mood was caffeinated and the mission was simple: find something vaguely wearable, have a laugh and maybe end the day feeling slightly less judgemental about the fashion industry.

That's when we stumbled upon it – a T-shirt hanging in the centre of a shop like some kind of sartorial punchline. It had a pair of breasts drawn on the front. Actual, cartoonishly round breasts, complete with perky nipples in strategic spots, like the T-shirt equivalent of a knowing wink.

My friend stopped dead in her tracks, squinting at the garment like it had personally insulted her. 'Is this ... fashion?' she asked, tilting her head.

'I think it's meant to be ironic,' I offered weakly, though I wasn't entirely sure.

'Ironic? So, what, we're supposed to buy a shirt with boobs on it because it's funny? Like, "Ha ha, I have these, and now they're on my shirt too"? What's next – pants with a dick drawn on them for men? Shall we ask the staff if they've got those in stock?'

At this point, I was laughing so hard that I had to lean on a nearby rack of denim shorts for support. 'Imagine! Men wandering around with trousers featuring a little chipolata or a zucchini print right across the crotch. Or maybe a banana if they're feeling particularly optimistic.'

'Oh, but women get breasts on T-shirts. How empowering!' she said, rolling her eyes so dramatically I was worried she'd injure herself.

After recovering from our shared hysteria, we decided to investigate this curious trend further. A quick walk around the shop confirmed that the fashion industry was, indeed, experiencing a full-blown obsession with boobs. There were shirts with melons, shirts with hearts strategically placed where breasts would be, and even one particularly disturbing number featuring two fried eggs.

'Fried eggs?' my friend said, holding it up in disbelief. 'Are they mocking small-breasted women now? "Oh, your chest is flat, so let's reduce it to breakfast."'

'Meanwhile,' I added, pointing to another rack, 'if you're on the fuller side, you can celebrate with a pair of watermelons. How generous of them to give us all such inclusive food metaphors for our bodies.'

We debated whether the whole thing was some kind of

ironic feminist statement: 'Love your body, embrace your boobs, let them be free!' Or perhaps it was an elaborate joke at women's expense – an industry-wide nudge-nudge-wink-wink moment designed to remind us that no matter how enlightened we think we've become, we're still just reduced to our anatomy.

I couldn't help but imagine how these shirts would play out in real life. Women already have to battle to get men to look into their eyes during conversations; imagine adding a visual pun to the mix. 'Ha ha, look at my melons!' one of these shirts practically screamed. 'Get it? Do you GET IT?'

It's bad enough that many women feel like walking billboards for the male gaze. Why on earth would anyone voluntarily slap a pair of cartoon breasts on their chest, effectively pointing out what the men were already staring at?

The irony of it all, of course, is that men would never wear the male equivalent. You don't see them parading around in trousers decorated with phallic symbols, do you? And before anyone suggests it's because men don't face the same kind of objectification as women – fair point – even if they did, I doubt they'd join in with the kind of gusto women are expected to muster.

My friend nodded solemnly. 'We're not exactly seeing guys stroll down the street in shirts that say, "Check out my pecs!" with two giant arrows pointing at their nipples.'

'Come to think of it ... I think the Italian prime minister's surname is Meloni – melons – and she did some sort of TikTok parody holding melons for breasts,' I mused.

My friend snorted with laughter.

But beneath the laughter, we both felt a certain weariness. Why was it that women, no matter how far we've come, are still reduced to parts of our bodies? Breasts aren't even the most interesting thing about us, for goodness' sake! Sure, they're functional, sometimes fun and occasionally inconvenient (any breastfeeding mother can attest to that), but are they really deserving of their current status as the most celebrated body part in fashion?

'Honestly,' my friend said, still chuckling but with a hint of exasperation, 'it's not even empowering. It's just lazy. If you want to celebrate breasts, do it properly. Write a poem. Build a statue. Don't slap a pair of fried eggs on a shirt and call it a revolution.'

'Exactly,' I said, in agreement. 'If we're going to celebrate our anatomy, let's at least do it with a bit more class.'

We left the store shortly after, feeling both amused and slightly annoyed. The T-shirt had sparked a conversation we hadn't expected but one that felt strangely necessary. It wasn't just about fashion – it was about how women are seen, how we see ourselves and whether we really need the approval of an industry that thinks breasts are the pinnacle of our existence.

As we walked back out into the sunshine, we passed a group of men, one of whom was wearing a T-shirt with the words 'King of the Grill' emblazoned across the chest. My friend gave me a sidelong glance.

'Well,' she said, 'at least they're sticking to barbecue humour. Small mercies.'

I laughed and hooked my arm through hers. 'Come on.

Let's find somewhere to have a drink and pretend the world makes sense.'

And as we clinked our glasses over a shared plate of fries, we couldn't help but marvel at the absurdity of it all. Fashion may come and go, but the nonsense stays the same.

• • •

CHAPTER ELEVEN

Madonna, Jean Paul Gaultier and conical bras

When Madonna strapped herself into Jean Paul Gaultier's pink satin cone bra during her 1990 Blond Ambition Tour, the world collectively gasped, snickered and, for some, clutched their pearls. This wasn't just an outfit; it was a battle cry. A declaration of independence. A sartorial middle finger to the rigid expectations of femininity, decorum and even gravity. It was Madonna at her finest: provocative, irreverent and absolutely unforgettable.

The cone bra itself – part corset, part postmodern art piece – managed to turn the idea of lingerie, something traditionally associated with the male gaze, into something weaponised. The cone bra represented a departure from soft female curves and was reimagined as a sharp weapon. This wasn't just an accessory; it was a weapon in the war for autonomy.

Gaultier's creation wasn't pulled out of a vacuum. The cone bra riffed on his longstanding fascination with lingerie-as-outerwear, a hallmark of his work since the 1980s. But while the Parisian designer's take on the corset initially conjured images of boudoir chic, Madonna transformed it into an icon. She didn't merely wear the bra – she inhabited it. Her gyrating hips, unapologetic stares and commanding stage presence made it clear: this wasn't about your pleasure, dear audience; it was about hers.

If the cone bra had spoken, it probably would have sounded something like Madonna herself: loud, unapologetic and slightly terrifying. It heralded a new era in which women could take the symbols of their objectification and wield them as tools of empowerment. Madonna's cone bra wasn't 'sexy' in the traditional sense. Its pointed architecture was downright menacing, an aesthetic weapon aimed at dismantling outdated notions of womanhood.

The Blond Ambition Tour was a carefully orchestrated carnival of excess, and the pink cone bra was its ringmaster. Every detail of Madonna's performance was calculated to shock and awe, but the bra served as the centrepiece – a wearable manifesto. It complemented the show's themes of religious iconography and sexual liberation, and the sometimes uncomfortable intersection of the two. In one moment, she'd be writhing on a bed, wearing the cone bra like a bulletproof vest; in the next, she'd don a priest's cassock over it, blending sacrilege with sensuality in ways that made the Vatican reach for its smelling salts.

Of course, the cone bra's cultural resonance extended far beyond the tour. It became a meme before memes existed, referenced and parodied endlessly. It graced magazine covers, inspired runway collections and cemented Madonna's status as a fashion icon. It also set a precedent for the high-fashion-meets-pop-star collaborations that dominate today's music industry. Without Gaultier's cone bra, would we have had Lady Gaga's meat dress or Beyoncé's Givenchy latex? Unlikely.

Critics and audiences alike struggled to categorise the cone bra. Was it feminist or anti-feminist? Empowering or exploitative? High art or lowbrow gimmickry? The answer, as with most things Madonna, was all of the above. The cone bra embodied the contradictions of femininity: nurturing yet aggressive, alluring yet intimidating. It didn't just blur the line between masculine and feminine; it obliterated it.

And let's not forget the sheer absurdity of the thing. The cone bra was ridiculous, and Madonna revelled in that ridiculousness. She understood that fashion didn't have to be serious to be powerful. By donning something so outrageous, she reminded us that gender, sexuality and power are all, to some extent, performances. The cone bra was both costume and critique, a joke with a razor-sharp punchline.

In hindsight, it's astonishing that something as seemingly frivolous as a pink satin bra could carry such weight. But Madonna has always had a knack for turning the banal into the iconic. She took Gaultier's design and turned a piece of lingerie into a symbol of rebellion. The cone bra was an outfit *and* a philosophy.

And yet, it wasn't universally adored. Critics dismissed it as vulgar; some fans found it alienating. Feminists debated whether it was a step forward or backward. The pearl-clutching reactionaries of the world, predictably, labelled it an abomination. But Madonna thrived on that discomfort. She didn't want universal approval; she wanted a reaction. In that sense, the cone bra was a resounding success.

Today, the cone bra sits in a museum, a relic of an era when pop stars weren't afraid to provoke. But its legacy lives on in the way artists use fashion to make statements. From Rihanna's sheer gowns to Lizzo's unapologetically bold ensembles, the spirit of the cone bra endures. It's a reminder that clothes can be more than just fabric; they can be weapons, shields and megaphones.

Jean Paul Gaultier once described his work as an attempt to 'liberate' women from the constraints of fashion. With the cone bra, he didn't just liberate – he annihilated. And in Madonna, he found the perfect muse. Together, they created a garment that was as much about challenging societal norms as it was about celebrating individuality.

Perhaps the ultimate irony of the cone bra is that, for all its sharp angles and provocative intent, it's also deeply nostalgic. Its design harks back to the bullet bras of the 1950s, an era when women's fashion was tightly controlled and rigidly defined. By reimagining this retro silhouette through a feminist, punk lens, Gaultier and Madonna turned a symbol of repression into one of liberation.

The cone bra: a ridiculous, fabulous, groundbreaking piece of fashion history. And if it made you think, or even feel a little uncomfortable?

Well, that was the point.

• • •

CHAPTER TWELVE

Breast politics

Breasts have been front and centre in the culture wars for, oh, about the last 50 years. First, you had the bra-burning 1970s, with second-wave feminists tossing away their undergarments in protest, because why *not* make an explosive statement with something so ... supportively constricting? Then came the ongoing, endlessly judgy debates about breastfeeding. Is it public? Is it private? Does it need a whole debate? And don't even get me started on the more recent squabbles over trans healthcare, which have made the humble breast an even more hotly contested battlefield.

Meanwhile, in a somewhat ironic twist, we have the modern age of Free the Nipple, hot girl summers and body positivity, where the girlies are proudly celebrating their breasts as symbols of freedom, power and sensuality. Sure, on Instagram, everyone's all about liberation and nipple freedom – 'Look at me, I'm so empowered in my bikini selfie!' But ask yourself: when was the last time you saw someone strutting around town with their nips out in broad daylight? Yeah, didn't think so.

Breasts are still the ultimate enigma: stuffed into bras, concealed under layers but still somehow constantly up for debate. Why are they so divisive? Perhaps it's because they represent a weird mishmash of everything: gender, sex, motherhood, politics and the very concept of 'How much skin is too much?' They're like a messy cocktail of emotions, desires and social rules we can't seem to shake, no matter how many hashtags we create.

They are the great feminist battleground. Breasts are both celebrated and scrutinised, fetishised and censored, worshipped and weaponised. As the saying goes: 'Behind every great woman is a pair of boobs trying desperately to stay out of the conversation.'

But the question remains: what *is* the feminist stance on boobs? And can it ever truly be resolved without laughing (and crying) into our underwire bras?

The evolution of the boob debate

It all starts in the Stone Age. Picture cavewomen roaming around freely, their breasts doing whatever prehistoric breasts did, blissfully unaware of the patriarchal nonsense to come. Fast-forward a few millennia and boobs are everywhere – Greek statues, Renaissance paintings and, eventually, *Sports Illustrated* covers.

By the 1960s, feminism had roared onto the scene and said, 'Hang on a minute, are we really going to let boobs define us?' Enter the bra-burning myths. No, feminists didn't actually torch their bras en masse (fires are dangerous and bras are expensive), but they did question whether society's obsession with perfectly perky cleavage was holding women back.

The debate hasn't cooled since. On one hand, boobs

are hailed as symbols of feminine power – Madonna's cone bra – and on the other hand, they're dismissed as the ultimate distraction, reducing women to little more than walking, talking chest regions. Feminists everywhere are left wondering: to free the nipple or not to free the nipple?

Boobs as power: The Wonderbra revolution

Let's talk about the Wonderbra, arguably feminism's greatest frenemy. A push-up bra of sorts, which promised to give you pert boobs even if you didn't have any, the Wonderbra burst onto the scene in the 1990s with ads promising to 'give women confidence' and 'empower them in the workplace'. Because, obviously, nothing says 'equal pay' like cleavage that could double as a coin slot.

Was the Wonderbra liberating or objectifying? Feminists couldn't agree. On one hand, it gave women control over their presentation – a literal boost to their self-esteem. On the other, it reinforced the idea that women's worth was tied to how high and mighty their boobs sat.

But let's be honest: even Gloria Steinem probably glanced in a mirror at some point and thought, 'Damn, this looks good.'

Free the Nipple: Progress or PR stunt?

In the 2010s, a new feminist boob revolution emerged. 'Free the Nipple' campaigners insisted that women should be able to go topless in public, just as men did. At first glance, it seemed like a no-brainer. Why should society police women's nipples while letting men's roam free? But then came the Instagram wars. Social media platforms, terrified of the female nipple's supposed power to destroy civilisation, began censoring any and all boob-related content.

Ironically, this censorship only made the movement stronger. Feminists argued that nipples – whether attached to a man or a woman – are just nipples. They're not inherently sexual; they're just there, like elbows or earlobes. (Though honestly, no one's starting a Free the Earlobe campaign, which feels like a missed opportunity.)

But the debate raged on. Some feminists applauded Free the Nipple as a step towards equality. Others rolled their eyes and said, 'We've got bigger fish to fry – like, you know, dismantling the patriarchy.'

Boobs in the workplace: A double-edged sword

Let's take the conversation to the office. If you're a woman in the workplace, you've probably had a moment where your boobs entered the chat – whether you wanted them to or not.

Wear a high-necked blouse? You're a prude. Opt for a V-neck? You're 'asking for it'. God forbid your bra strap peeks out during a meeting – HR will be at your desk faster than you can say 'corporate feminism'.

It's a lose-lose situation. Feminists argue that women should be able to dress however they like without their competence being questioned. But societal norms are stubborn, and boobs remain a workplace conundrum.

The solution? Many women adopt the 'ignore and conquer' strategy: wear what you want, walk into the boardroom and let your PowerPoint presentation do the talking. If someone's still focused on your chest, that's their problem – not yours.

Breastfeeding in public: The ultimate double standard

Ah, breastfeeding. The act of nourishing a tiny human with your body – and somehow still a subject of public outrage.

Feminists have long rallied behind the right of women to breastfeed in public, arguing that it's a natural, beautiful process that shouldn't be shamed. Critics, meanwhile, mutter about 'modesty' and 'decency', as if a woman feeding her baby is somehow more offensive than, say, a beer ad featuring bikini-clad women bouncing on a trampoline.

The irony is almost too much to bear. Breasts are plastered across billboards and music videos, celebrated as symbols of desire. But the moment they're used for their biological purpose, everyone suddenly loses their minds.

The boob-job dilemma: Feminist or faux pas?

Now, let's address the elephant in the room – or, rather, the augmentations. Is getting a boob job anti-feminist? Is my good friend Amanda profoundly anti-feminist?

The answer, as with most feminist debates, is: it's complicated.

On one hand, surgically altering your body to fit

societal beauty standards feels like giving in to patriarchal pressure. On the other, feminism is about choice – and if a boob job makes you feel confident and empowered, who's to judge?

The real question is: who are you doing it for? If it's for yourself, many feminists say, go for it. But if it's to meet someone else's expectations, it might be time to re-evaluate.

Boobs and the male gaze: A never-ending saga

At the heart of the feminist boob debate lies the infamous 'male gaze'. Feminists argue that much of society's obsession with breasts stems from how men perceive them – as objects of desire, rather than parts of a whole person.

The male gaze is why ads for everything from hamburgers to car insurance feature impossibly perfect cleavage. It's why women's nipples are censored on social media, while men's are not. It's why, even today, boobs are still treated as public property for comment and critique.

The feminist response? Reclaim the narrative. Boobs aren't just for men's enjoyment – they're ours, to do with as we please. Wear a low-cut dress, go braless or rock a turtleneck. The choice is yours, and that's what matters.

The final word on feminist boobs

Feminism isn't a monolith, so the feminist stance on boobs is not a simple one. Some feminists see boobs as a symbol of oppression; others view them as a source of power. Most agree on one thing: women should have the freedom to exist - boobs and all - without being reduced to their chest size.

At the end of the day, boobs are just boobs. They're a body part, like any other. They're not inherently feminist or anti-feminist - they're just there, doing their thing.

And maybe that's the ultimate feminist stance: to stop overthinking boobs entirely. To let them be what they are - soft, squishy and occasionally annoying - and focus on the bigger picture.

Because, let's face it, we've got more important things to fight for. Like equal pay. And universal childcare. And, you know, world peace.

• • •

CHAPTER THIRTEEN

'Why are you so scared of breasts?'

When actor Florence Pugh shared photos of herself in a pink Valentino gown on Instagram in 2022, she likely anticipated a variety of reactions. The gown, sheer enough to proudly reveal her breasts, was celebrated by some as a statement of liberation and confidence. Others, however, flooded her comments with criticism and insults, fixating on her choice to forgo a bra and framing her body as a site of public debate. It wasn't long before the conversation spiralled into a predictable mix of misogyny, body shaming and moral panic.

The sheer volume of vitriol Pugh received highlighted just how uncomfortable society remains with women who defy unspoken rules about how their bodies should be displayed. In response, she addressed the criticism head-on, posing a direct question to her detractors: 'Why are you so scared of breasts?' This simple but cutting inquiry underscored the absurdity of the outrage surrounding her choice of attire.

Her question, though addressed to the predominantly male critics in her comments, carried broader implications.

It was a challenge to a culture that simultaneously worships and fears the female body – a culture that demands women conform to narrow ideals while vilifying them when they refuse. Pugh's boldness in refusing to apologise for her body forces us to confront why something as ordinary as breasts continues to provoke such intense discomfort.

The fear of breasts can manifest as outright misogyny, or as the more insidious forms of body policing present in content-moderation algorithms. On social media platforms like Instagram, where visual culture thrives, this policing of women's bodies is starkly visible. While men's nipples are displayed freely, women's are deemed inappropriate, hypersexualised by default, and images of them are removed under the guise of preserving community standards.

Pugh's post challenged this double standard. Her photos, while unapologetic, were neither provocative nor overtly sexual. Yet they sparked the kind of backlash typically reserved for acts perceived as transgressive, like being naked in public – think Bianca Censori's nude look on the red carpet. It was part of a broader cultural contradiction: breasts are celebrated in advertising, entertainment and art when presented in ways that align with societal norms. But the moment they are displayed outside these carefully curated contexts, they become a problem to be patrolled. Pugh's refusal to accommodate this hypocrisy forced her audience to confront the arbitrariness of these unwritten rules.

The backlash Pugh received is not unique. Women who embrace their bodies in ways that deviate from societal expectations are often subjected to similar scrutiny. Instagram's history of enforcing its nudity policy disproportionately against women highlights how these standards become codified – turned into rules – for moderating content online. This extends beyond Pugh to impact marginalised communities even more acutely. Black, plus-sized and LGBTQIA+ creators are frequently penalised under policies that claim to uphold 'decency' but instead perpetuate existing biases. The 2020 removal of Nyome Nicholas-Williams' semi-nude photograph, which adhered to Instagram's guidelines but was still flagged for 'breast squeezing', exemplifies this disparity.

Pugh's position as a young, white, cisgender and conventionally attractive celebrity shields her from some of the harsher consequences of this cultural policing. She is able to speak out in ways that others cannot. However, it is significant that she is willing to use this privilege to challenge the status quo and amplify these conversations. By refusing to back down in the face of misogynistic criticism, Pugh aligns herself with a lineage of feminist figures who have fought to reclaim narratives around women's bodies.

Her response also touches on the broader mechanisms of control perpetuated by social media platforms. In her follow-up post, Pugh called attention to how easily men can destroy women's bodies publicly and without consequence, thanks to unchecked misogyny that flourishes online *and* the platforms themselves for enabling such behaviour. The algorithms and policies that govern social media create environments where women's bodies are disproportionately censored, perpetuating harmful beauty standards while silencing expressions of body positivity or defiance.

By engaging with these issues, Pugh brought a fresh perspective to this ongoing debate. For her, this wasn't just a conversation about censorship, but about society's obsession with controlling women's bodies. Her insistence that her body is her own, to present however she pleases, was a radical assertion of autonomy in a culture that persistently denies it.

Her defiance reminds us that the conversation is not just about the right to display a body part but about challenging the systems and norms that tell us how women 'should' exist in the world. Breasts are not inherently political, but the layers of meaning and control imposed upon them make them so. Pugh's approach – unapologetic, confident and unyielding – offers a blueprint for how to navigate these cultural battlegrounds. It's not just about freeing the nipple; it's about freeing women from the countless expectations and restrictions placed upon them.

In celebrating her own body, Pugh made space for others to do the same. Her advocacy, while grounded in her personal experience, resonated because it tapped into a universal struggle for autonomy and respect. The question of why society remains so obsessed with policing women's breasts is ultimately a question about control, power and fear. And by daring to confront that fear, Florence Pugh challenges us all to do the same.

• • •

CHAPTER FOURTEEN

Men, boobs and art

Breasts in art: a tale as old as time. Or at least as old as the Venus of Willendorf, a pint-sized prehistoric icon who's been flexing her fertility power moves for 30,000 years. This Venus is a portable Palaeolithic female figurine discovered in Austria in 1908. With her oversized, unapologetic boobs, she basically screamed, 'Life starts here, folks!' If cave-dwellers had had Instagram, she'd have been the first body-positive influencer.

But while men have long been leaving their mark on public spaces with phallic graffiti – desks, walls, the literal sky – breasts have dominated the *high* art world. Why? Well, the story of art is mostly the story of men. Men painting women. Men sculpting women. Men deciding what constitutes 'beauty'. Women, when they could create, often had to masquerade as men, or join a convent, all for the radical right to wield a paintbrush. And yet breasts, the universal icons of nurture and allure, have remained front and centre through millennia of artistic evolution.

We begin in the era of loincloths and mammoth steaks. The Venus of Willendorf was less about human anatomy and more about broadcasting fertility vibes. Those giant breasts weren't saying, 'Hey, look at me' so much as

'I can survive a famine *and* pop out a few kids.' Practicality, prehistoric-style.

By the time the Egyptians got their hieroglyphs going, breasts had taken on a different tone. Sure, queens and goddesses got their spotlight, but it was all very tasteful. Think functional, not flirty. Isis, the OG multitasking mum, is often depicted breastfeeding her son Horus – a divine milk bar, if you will. The takeaway? Breasts were sacred, like an ancient gift card to the gods.

Then the Greeks and Romans entered, chiselled marble in hand, and said, 'Let's make this sexy.' They cranked up the aesthetic dial, presenting breasts as impossibly symmetrical and gravity defying. (Clearly, they hadn't met reality yet.) Aphrodite, the goddess of love, often showed up topless in statues, reminding everyone that beauty was her full-time job. Meanwhile, Roman artists added literal breastplates to warrior goddesses because even divinity had to multitask as both nurturing and combative.

Fast-forward to medieval Europe, where breasts got a PR rebrand: modesty central. The Virgin Mary cornered the market on breast representation, her bosom seen as a vessel of divine nourishment. Art at the time leaned into the whole 'pure and nurturing' vibe. Breasts were on display but under strict terms – no sensuality allowed, thank you very much. (Unless you count some of those oddly curious cherubs.)

Cue the Renaissance, where the floodgates of boob appreciation burst open. Botticelli's *The Birth of Venus* practically glows with soft curves and sultry confidence. Breasts in this era didn't whisper; they proclaimed,

'Beauty is back, baby!' Portraits of noblewomen leaned into plunging necklines, signalling a newfound celebration of the human form and individuality. Breasts had gone mainstream, and the vibe was both elegant and a little saucy.

Then came the Baroque period, where everything got extra. More voluptuous, more dramatic, more emotionally intense. Caravaggio painted breasts with the kind of gritty realism that said, 'Yep, this is what they actually look like.' It was all very visceral, making viewers squirm with the raw humanity of it all. Breasts were no longer distant ideals; they were flesh and blood, imperfect and alive.

By the 18th and 19th centuries, breasts became revolutionary icons. Literally. Eugène Delacroix's *Liberty Leading the People* gave us Liberty herself, bare-breasted and waving the tricolour flag. Her exposed bosom screamed freedom, rebellion and maternal care – a revolutionary trifecta. Meanwhile, neoclassicism brought back the Greek vibes but with a polished, hyper-idealised twist. Breasts were symbols of virtue, elegance and, occasionally, an excuse to justify elaborate togas.

Then modern art showed up, ready to smash every convention. Pablo Picasso took the female form and rearranged it into something only vaguely recognisable, turning breasts into abstract geometry. Meanwhile, surrealists like Salvador Dalí gave us dreamlike, sometimes unsettling interpretations – breasts as drawers, clocks or anything but breasts. Feminist artists, on the other hand, reclaimed the narrative, using breasts as symbols of empowerment and defiance. Judy Chicago and her peers transformed them into canvases for exploring identity, autonomy and societal expectations. Art wasn't just about seeing breasts; it was about rethinking them.

But let's talk Picasso and Dalí – and misogyny – later.

Today, breasts in art are as diverse as the world itself. Hyperrealistic portraits sit alongside digital installations and Instagram-worthy body-positivity campaigns. They're symbols of beauty, nourishment, power and protest. They challenge norms, spark conversations and remain central to the way we express humanity. Whether they're abstracted, idealised or lovingly detailed, breasts are an enduring testament to the complexities of art – and the human condition.

• • •

CHAPTER FIFTEEN

As if I was going to stop at one ...

Amanda

I'm not going to go into how I became Samantha X, Australia's most high-profile escort. If you didn't know already and this is all news to you, no doubt you have lots of questions. But I've written about it at length in my three books (the latest is called *Misfit*).

There are many complex reasons I became an escort, but this is the short version: for about a year after my relationship ended, I dated a few men. After many disappointments, at age 37 I decided that if a man was going to waste my time, he was going to pay for it – with money. Lots and lots of money. $1500 an hour, to be exact.

And I loved it. The thrill, the excitement, the hotels, the travel and the money. Definitely the money.

And that money I used to pay my bills and my mortgage, to support my young kids and to have plenty in the bank for ... plastic surgery. (And tax, of course.)

I'm going to gloss over the next decade. You don't need to know about the highs, the lows, the partying, the ups and the downs. It was quite the ride. But what you ought to know, seeing this is about a book about boobs, is that in the decade of Samantha X, I had about five boob jobs.

I was quite content with my little (bigger) boobs from my first operation until I met a 'fellow lady of the night'. Let's call her Jet. Jet was stunning: long, shiny black hair; glossy, plump red lips; stunning figure. And ... huge boobs. I met her in the agency I was working for and fell in love (or lust) with her enviable figure. She was the most popular girl at the agency, known as the night-time party girl. I was probably seen as more of a girl next door, someone who could be your friendly work colleague – perfect for the 'girlfriend' experience.

'Oh, baby,' Jet breathed huskily at me in her Russian accent, after I asked her what size her boobs were. 'You seriously expect me to remember? I've had so many boob jobs.'

'What? I just had one ...'

She laughed. 'Oh, baby, you've only had *one*? Wait till you have your second, third and fourth. It will never be enough. You will get bigger and bigger ...'

Wow. I suddenly felt *really* girl-next-door with my boring mousy-brown hair and sensible, socially acceptable and – now, in my eyes – small boobs.

I hadn't even realised you could have more than one boob job, that you could just go bigger and bigger and bigger until you had huge sexy boobs like that hot Russian escort. Just like I didn't realise you could stop at one drink, or you could even say no to a drink, it didn't occur to me that I could get another boob job. I had the money, the time, the desire, the greed, the vanity and certainly the insecurity. So why the fuck not? It was as easy as that! *My life will be perfect*, I thought, *absolutely perfect, if I have bigger boobs.*

So back I went to see Dr Liew. Again, don't ask me the year, how old I was or what size I chose. I think it was a 600cc, which is a large D, and I was about 41 years old. I *think*. I do remember the pain wasn't as bad, probably because my skin had already been stretched from boob job number one, and that the recovery was easier.

And I do remember the looks, the glances of men, their faces lighting up as they gave me the once-over, gliding their eyes from my eyes to my chest with lightning speed. I remember having a portfolio of escort photos shot, with my boobs bursting out of the sexy lingerie. I felt sexy and powerful. I felt desirable. It wasn't just clients – I honestly think they didn't give a shit. Believe it or not, my job as Samantha X was more therapy than sex. It was anonymous men, in the street, in the supermarket, in cafes, who gave me that little buzz of validation and approval. And it was all down to the size of my breasts.

That wasn't enough. A few years later, I went under the knife again, at around age 45. And I went *big*: 800cc. A *big* E. I was becoming addicted to the feeling of power it gave me.

That's right: power. The size of my chest was giving me power and, just like I had become addicted to the champagne, the money, the thrill, the clients and the notoriety of being Samantha X, I was fast becoming addicted to the power of being blonde with big tits.

• • •

CHAPTER SIXTEEN

Small-breasted women are sophisticated

I was at my desk, tapping away at my computer, ignoring the animated chatter in the background. The younger women in the office were discussing their weekends, the new cafes they'd discovered and the outfits they were planning for upcoming parties and dinners. I couldn't help but overhear bits and pieces of their conversation. My concentration was only broken when one of them, a bright-eyed twenty-something, declared:

'I'm going to buy the Skims shapewear.'

Skims. Ah, yes. The Kardashian-approved shapewear line, which has infiltrated every corner of social media like an uninvited guest at a fancy dinner party. For those of you who have been living under a rock – or, like me, are blissfully ignorant of certain cultural phenomena – Skims is Kim Kardashian's shapewear brand. It's a line of products designed to shape, lift and tuck you into perfection without you needing an entire wardrobe overhaul. For those who are in the know, it's the go-to brand for creating that 'smooth, snatched look' that is apparently now the gold standard.

'I love Skims!' another voice piped up, with that eager tone that only the truly obsessed can muster.

'What about her new bra with built-in nipples?' a man in the corner interjected, as though he'd just stumbled upon the most groundbreaking invention since the wheel.

'I know, hilarious,' came the response, as if the very idea of built-in nipples was the pinnacle of comedic brilliance.

I didn't know where to look. This conversation was getting increasingly bizarre. The built-in nipple bra? Really? And why was this such a big deal?

But, of course, I was the old one in the office, the one who didn't understand these things, the one whose experiences hadn't been shaped by the wonders of TikTok or Kardashian culture. I was the dinosaur who had lived through the era of push-up bras and unspeakably uncomfortable wire frames. Not to mention that I had always been under the impression that nipples were, you know, *natural*.

'Lisa, what do you think?' they asked me, as they always did. I wasn't sure if they genuinely wanted my opinion or if they just found my responses so hilariously out of step with everything they knew. Either way, they always seemed to enjoy it when I weighed in on these topics. Mostly because, I think, my views came across as a bit like your grandma trying to operate an iPhone: delightfully confused and inadvertently funny.

I turned slightly, trying my best to look like a person who understood the cultural nuances of the younger generation. 'What do I think about shapewear?' I began, then paused, searching for the right words. 'What do I think about bras with built-in nipples?' I spun around dramatically in my chair like a cartoon villain, preparing to drop some wisdom on them.

'I need more than a bra with nipples,' I said, deadpan. 'I need a bra with boobs built into it.'

The entire office erupted into laughter.

'Stop it! You have such a nice aesthetic. Like, a Frenchwoman's aesthetic,' Lucy declared, with a grin.

I blinked. 'A Frenchwoman's aesthetic?' What on earth was that? Another TikTok trend that had somehow passed me by?

'Yeah, like the French actress in *Emily in Paris*, you know the one who runs the PR agency?' Lucy said, her eyes shining as if she'd just bestowed upon me a compliment of the highest order.

I had no idea what was happening, but I nodded like I understood. *Emily in Paris* was some Netflix show in which Lily Collins' character Emily – who seemed to have a perpetual look of surprise – moved to France and immersed herself in a world of high fashion, countless boyfriends and absurd plotlines. Oh, and she was somehow a PR genius at the ripe old age of 29 despite having no experience in the field. The French actress Lucy was referring to was the effortlessly chic, rail-thin Philippine Leroy-Beaulieu, who played a French PR mogul with the ability to condescend with just a raised eyebrow. Yes, I knew the one.

'French chic,' Lucy continued, as if it were a universally accepted term.

I was starting to feel like I'd stepped into an alternate universe. 'Really?' I asked, my inner feminist on full alert.

The room buzzed with laughter and approval. Lucy had found my aesthetic. She'd defined it for me. Apparently, I was 'French chic', which I could only assume meant I was stylish, I was thin and I had a deep disdain for anything Anglo-Saxon. How could I resist such a flattering label?

'Well,' I said, feigning a little hesitation, 'I've been thinking about getting my breasts done.'

The room went silent.

'*What?*' Lucy shrieked, like I'd just revealed that I was secretly a superhero with a dark alter ego.

'Why not?' I asked, genuinely curious. I didn't see why people would react so dramatically.

'Because there's a certain type of woman who gets her breasts done,' said Sara, who I would later learn was a self-proclaimed Coquette Girl (a particular aesthetic that gen Z adores), with a look of sheer horror on her face.

'A type?' I raised an eyebrow, already intrigued. 'What do you mean?'

'You know,' Sara continued, looking as though I'd just confessed to committing an unpardonable sin, 'like, lips filled with filler, hair extensions, and, uh ... OnlyFans accounts.'

Now I had to pause. *Wait a second.* I have extensions. Am I the 'type'? Was this a trap? Was I now an OnlyFans woman without even knowing it?

'I think a lot of women get their boobs done,' I countered, unsure of what was about to happen, my voice shaking slightly.

'Only the ones that do porn,' one of the guys chimed in from the corner.

I rolled my eyes and slowly turned back to my desk. The men. They always had to weigh in on women's business, didn't they?

'You're so sophisticated,' Lucy continued, completely ignoring the chaos I had just caused. 'You're not the "boob job type".' She said this as though she had just made a profound observation.

Sophisticated? *Me?* Well, I'll take that compliment – despite the fact that I was currently in my oversized cardigan, with frizzy hair and no makeup. But I could feel the underlying assumption that big boobs were, well, unsophisticated.

'Are small boobs sophisticated?' I asked out loud, more to stir the pot than anything.

The room went quiet for a moment, before Coquette Girl jumped in. 'With small boobs, you do look better in clothes.'

And then, as though they'd rehearsed it, everyone chimed in.

'You do!'

'Small boobs are just better.'

'With big boobs, you look fat in everything,' Christine, the only woman with actual breasts in the office, declared with alarming confidence.

The others, of course, disagreed. 'No you don't!' they protested, all shaking their heads vigorously. Body-positivity movement in full swing.

But Christine was insistent. 'Prepare to buy a whole new wardrobe if you get your boobs done,' she warned me, as if she were some fashion oracle predicting my fate.

And then Lucy, ever the diplomat, added, 'Well, I guess with small boobs, you're more of a clothes horse.'

'Oh, *less droopage*,' the male designer quipped, clearly trying to inject his opinion into the conversation.

Cue the collective women's outrage. 'Shut up, Luke!' they all shouted in unison, like a well-coordinated chant.

'More like your balls will droop,' Lucy added, raising her eyebrows like she'd just dropped the mic.

With that, the conversation came to a resounding close. According to the wisdom of my co-workers, porn stars get big boobs and small boobs are inherently sophisticated. That was the takeaway.

And thus, I learned that in the strange, TikTok-driven world of today, breasts are not just body parts. No, no. They are symbols, power dynamics and aesthetic statements. They can determine whether you're sophisticated or, apparently, a porn star. It was all very 'French chic' – minus the 'drooping balls' comment, of course.

• • •

CHAPTER SEVENTEEN

Only escorts have their boobs done

After picking up my 18-month-old from my mother-in-law's place that evening, I called Amanda from the car. I couldn't wait to recount the absurd office breast innuendo I'd been subjected to earlier. The whole conversation had been an eye-opener, a hilarious dive into the weird and wonderful world of modern-day breast aesthetics.

'So, you will not believe what happened at work today,' I started, easing into the conversation as I navigated the familiar streets, my baby in the back seat babbling away.

'Oh, I'm already intrigued,' Amanda said, her voice a mix of amusement and curiosity.

'Well, there was this whole discussion about boobs – big boobs, small boobs, implants, you name it. Apparently, small breasts are considered "sophisticated". Like, that's the new thing. But here's the kicker – someone said that only porn stars get their boobs done.'

Amanda burst into laughter. 'What? Only porn stars? Well, that's news to me! I used to think only escorts got their boobs done. I swear, I would sit in the waiting room at the surgeon's office and look around thinking, *You're an escort, you're an escort, you're* definitely *an escort.*' She laughed again. 'But now, every second woman has implants. The place is full of perfectly normal women. It's wild.'

'Yeah, I know what you mean,' I replied. 'It's so strange how things have changed. I've never actually been to a breast consultation myself, but I know plenty of women who aren't in any way in the adult industry and still have breast implants.'

'Exactly!' Amanda said. 'It's like we've normalised the whole thing. Breast augmentation is as common as getting a haircut. But it wasn't always like this, was it? It used to be something that was kind of ... taboo. Something only the boldest women dared to do. I think your colleagues are off the mark.'

I sighed. 'They're gen Z ...'

'... puritans,' she filled in the blank.

'Exactly,' I said, shaking my head as I pictured the women in the surgeon's waiting room. 'There is so much pressure these days for your body to look a certain way. Every centimetre of it!'

'You should come with me,' Amanda said, out of nowhere.

'Come with you where?' I asked, momentarily distracted by a toddler tantrum in the back seat.

'To my consult with Doctor Moradi. You know, to have my breasts reduced,' she said casually, as though she were just discussing a dentist appointment.

'You're really going through with it?' I asked, surprised.

Amanda had mentioned before that she was planning on having her implants reduced, replacing her 1050cc ones – the largest size in the range – with something smaller. But she had been wavering on the decision, torn between wanting to downsize and not wanting to part with the big boobs she'd come to rely on. It was a classic case of 'breast tension', as I liked to call it.

'Yep, it's booked,' Amanda confirmed. 'But I still don't know if I should go to fifty per cent or seventy per cent of what they are now. I'm stuck.'

'Seventy,' I said without hesitation. 'Otherwise, it might be too much of a shock.'

'I don't know ...' she mused, clearly not convinced. 'I just feel like I'm so over these big boobs. They're ridiculous. But at the same time, I'm scared I'm going to lose all my power. I've had these things for so long, I don't know what it's going to be like to go smaller. It's like I'm losing a part of myself.'

'I hear you,' I said sympathetically. I knew that Amanda had lived with her large breasts for years, and I could see how they'd become part of her identity. But I also knew how uncomfortable she'd been with them at times. I had to agree that going smaller wasn't just about practicality; it was about finding a new identity. And the fear of losing that power she mentioned? It was real.

'I had my hair done today in Bondi,' Amanda continued, clearly still processing the emotions tied up in the decision. 'And this woman walked in with implants, we started talking, and she was a yogi. I told her I was getting my breasts reduced, and she told me hers had gotten infected, but she would rather die than have them removed. Can you believe that?'

'Wow. That's intense,' I replied, my mind reeling. 'What makes her so attached to them? I mean, infection is serious! Why would anyone go through it if it's making them sick?'

'I don't know,' Amanda said, her voice taking on a more serious tone. 'It's like these implants become a part of you, almost like an extension of your identity. I read an article the other day that said women with breast implants are more likely to commit suicide than women without them. Isn't that crazy?'

'Wait, what? Suicide?' I said, trying to process what she was saying. 'That's so heavy. I had no idea. Do they know why?'

Amanda was quiet for a moment. 'It's the pressure,' she said softly. 'The pressure to be perfect, to have these huge breasts, and the constant attention. It's overwhelming for some women. And when you can't live up to this ideal anymore, it messes with your head.

'And then you get these tits and you think your life is going to be perfect but actually nothing changes. You're still the same person.'

'Wow, I can't even imagine what that's like,' I said, my mind racing. Breasts had never been a point of obsession for me. But this new world I was being introduced to – this world of breast augmentation, reduction and identity tied to size – was starting to feel so much more intense than I could've ever imagined.

'Do you want to come with me to the consult? I think it'd be fun,' Amanda said again, offering me a chance to be a part of this personal moment. It was a generous invitation, given the nature of the consultation and how private it would be. But Amanda wasn't just thoughtful; she was a storyteller. She knew that the drama surrounding breasts – whether big or small – would make for some good conversation. And who wouldn't want to be a part of that?

'Sure, I'd love to,' I responded.

Why not? It was clear that *everyone* needed a breast consult these days.

• • •

CHAPTER EIGHTEEN

Pamela Anderson: Only invited to the Met Gala after she stopped wearing makeup

We were on a Zoom call, the kind in which you can't escape the awkwardness of trying to pretend your wi-fi connection is strong enough for you to be a decent participant. On one side of the screen, there was Amanda, looking effortlessly chic as always. On the other were two producers who had been working on a version of her life – a series that would one day feature dramatic re-enactments of her carefully curated Instagram life.

The topic of discussion, of course, was who would play Amanda in the show. Everyone had an opinion. People's lives were being distilled into an idea of someone else: how could an actress possibly embody her essence? This was not just about capturing the nuances of her personality, it was about finding someone who could translate her 'brand' onto the screen – physically, emotionally and, of course, in terms of ... well, size.

'It has to be an actress with big boobs,' the male

producer said, leaning forward in his chair. He was earnest, his face serious. 'Like really big boobs. That's her defining feature.' He gestured toward Amanda's image on the screen.

I felt the cold sweat of impending discomfort settle in. Were we really about to have this conversation? Could we not just pick someone who could act? I kept quiet for a moment, wondering if I could possibly remain neutral and just observe how this awkward conversation would unfold.

'Like a Pamela Anderson type,' the producer continued, completely unaware of the depth of my internal eye roll, 'but someone who can actually act.'

I hit pause in my mind. I loved that Pamela Anderson was being used as the benchmark. As if the only defining feature of Pamela Anderson's career was her body. Not her years of experience on *Baywatch* or the way she managed to become a media mogul in her own right, despite public opinion reducing her to a caricature. Notably, Anderson had recently come to critical acclaim via her role in *The Last Showgirl*. Perhaps she always could act? But okay, we were playing by those rules.

'I love Pamela Anderson,' Amanda cooed. I could see the playful smile on her face, as though she was mildly entertained by this whole ridiculousness.

'Oh, please.' Both producers simultaneously rolled their eyes. The simultaneous motion made it feel like I was watching an old-school sitcom in which everyone in the room suddenly becomes an exaggerated version of themselves.

'I love her too,' I chimed in, mainly because I couldn't resist the temptation to further drive the point home that *we* were the ones with the better taste.

'Oh, not you too!' the male producer groaned. 'How can anyone take her seriously?'

This was where I felt the familiar rise of annoyance. Who was he to say that Pamela Anderson couldn't be taken seriously? Sure, she had worked as a Playboy bunny, but so what? She wasn't the first and she definitely wouldn't be the last. If we were going to critique people's pasts and how they made their money, we'd all be in big trouble. Besides, her modern statement on beauty and her fresh face spoke to a reclaiming of identity not just for herself but for all women who had been sexualised.

'What do you mean, "Why can't we take her seriously?"' I countered, fully aware of where this conversation was about to go.

'She was a Playboy bunny who made her money as a result of her gigantic breasts. We can't take *Baywatch* seriously, or even consider it as acting.' The producer said this like it was a factual statement, as though everyone should agree.

'She's just released a best-selling autobiography. *And* been the subject of a hugely successful documentary. She was at the Met Gala, for crying out loud!' I retorted, pulling out all the stops, as though attending the Met Gala was some sort of undeniable validation of cultural importance.

'She was only invited to the Met Gala because she stopped wearing makeup,' the male producer said with a smug nod.

I felt my body physically recoil from the words. 'What does that mean?' I asked, genuinely baffled. The implications of what he was saying had layers, and none of them seemed to make sense.

'It means, the face is now supporting the feminist and fashion agendas,' he continued, his voice dripping with faux wisdom. 'And this counteracts the fact that the breasts are not.'

My jaw nearly hit the floor. 'The face is now supporting the feminist, fashion agenda?' I repeated, trying to make sense of the sentence that had just come out of his mouth.

'Yes, you know, the radical feminist sort of agenda,' he replied, as though it should all be clear to me now.

'And this is fashionable?' I quipped, testing his ability to see the irony of it all. I wasn't expecting an answer that made sense, but I needed to throw the ball back in their court.

'Yes.' He nodded vigorously.

'Or, at least, it's surprising,' the other producer added. And there they were, both of them, nodding in agreement like they had unlocked the secret to modern feminism with one swift observation about Pamela Anderson's post-makeup phase. I honestly felt like I needed a stiff drink, but that would have to wait.

'You see, she wasn't going to be invited to the Met as regular big-breasted Pammy. It's just so ... déclassé,' the female producer added, the words rolling off her tongue in the most pretentious way possible. 'It's not high fashion.'

Déclassé. I couldn't help but laugh internally. So, now Pamela Anderson's 'regular' self – big boobs, bleached blonde hair and a penchant for *Baywatch* reruns – was considered 'déclassé'. I was beginning to understand the level of cultural gatekeeping happening here. It was like some sort of social class warfare, with Pamela Anderson's legacy being reduced to nothing more than the size of her breasts.

'But now, she's writing books, supporting PETA, denouncing filmmakers who made series without her involvement and wearing no makeup. So, this counteracts the big boobs,' they both continued in unison, as though this was some sacred truth.

I didn't know whether to laugh or scream. 'Don't you see,' I began, my voice wild now with frustration, 'that the idea of going "makeup-free" is actually misleading? That it's so insidious? It hides all the costs, the labour, the artifice, the actual effort that goes into constructing this *no-makeup* look!'

They both stared at me, blankly. Amanda's eyes were wide, a kind of silent plea for help. I could tell she was over this conversation. I fumbled for my phone, knowing she had sent me a message.

Big boobs = déclassé, it read.

I laughed, despite myself. The irony was just too much. Here I was, trapped in a discussion about Pamela Anderson's breasts, her 'big boobs' and their supposed place in modern feminism, and all I could think was that the entire conversation was wrapped in layers of judgement, ignorance and misplaced priorities.

I put my phone down and glanced at the producers, who were still discussing the potential actresses they had in mind, each of them more invested in the 'big boobs = success' theory than I had anticipated. I had to admit, I was tired. It had been one of those days where everything seemed to hinge on the superficial – on things like breasts, faces and how one's body fit into a particular cultural narrative.

Amanda, however, was not one to be swayed by these conversations. She was laughing now, albeit nervously, but I could tell she was just as done with the conversation as I was. The producers, oblivious to the discomfort they'd caused, continued to brainstorm actresses who fit their idea of Amanda's 'look'. And me? I had learned that once again, the world seemed to be obsessed with fitting women into these tiny boxes, judging them by their size, their appearance and their past decisions, while forgetting all the complexities that made them who they truly were.

And Pamela Anderson? Well, she'd been reduced to a cultural symbol of something she would never quite escape. And yet I still couldn't help but admire the way she'd managed to rise above it all, despite everything. What a strange, strange world we live in.

• • •

CHAPTER NINETEEN

Big boobs, small boobs and the Madonna–Whore Complex

The Madonna–Whore Complex is a neat, tidy little box that places all women into one of two mutually exclusive categories: virginal, holy Madonna (yes, on this occasion we're talking about the Virgin Mary); or sinful, promiscuous Whore. It's a categorisation as old as time, as pervasive as air, and as delightfully ridiculous as that one aunt who insists that a woman can't wear a plunging neckline if she wants to be 'respectable'. It divides the female experience into two distinct, rigid compartments, as if women can't be simultaneously nurturing, wise, sexual and just a bit naughty.

This bizarre dichotomy was labelled by psychoanalyst Sigmund Freud as the 'Virgin–Whore Complex', and it has since permeated almost every corner of society. Freud observed it in his clinical work with men, noting that some were only able to have sex with prostitutes or mistresses because they were able to compartmentalise their sexual desires away from their moral reverence for their wives. To put it bluntly: men were sexually attracted to women they didn't respect and unable to feel sexual desire for women they did. Freud's conclusion? For men who exhibited this 'complex', women had to fit into one of two categories – pure, respected and untouched; or sexually available, dirty and unworthy of respect. It's a classic case of 'You can't respect women and want them at the same time', as if respect is the one thing standing in the way of male sexual desire.

Picture it: you've got the Madonna, with her quiet, demure presence, possibly small breasts, soft curves and an expression of piety. Maybe she's swaddling a baby (because what else is there for a woman to do?). Her small, 'quiet' breasts are symbolic of her purity, modesty and moral integrity. She is a passive vessel for the good, the pure, and – most importantly – the sexless. You see, for the Madonna, sexuality is a filthy, base thing that has no place under her shining halo. To have any sexual desire or even express sexual agency would be to shatter the delicate, saintly image that she embodies. If the Madonna had big breasts, it would ruin her entire aesthetic. Could you imagine the Virgin Mary with a busty, heaving chest? That would throw everything off. No, no. She must remain small, quiet and perfectly restrained in every sense, especially when it comes to her body. You want to be a good, respectable woman? Keep those breasts to yourself – modesty is the key.

And then there's the Whore – big-breasted, loud and unashamed. The Whore is everything the Madonna is not: sexually liberated, loud, and ready to claim her body as her own. Her large breasts (perhaps a bit more exaggerated than in real life, a little extra to draw attention) are symbols of abundance, sensuality and a complete rejection of the social norms that would demand she be quiet and demure. If the Madonna's small, quiet breasts signify her purity, the Whore's larger, more audacious breasts say, 'I'm here, I'm sexual, and you're going to notice.' The Whore embodies excess – excess of desire, of energy, of life itself. She refuses to hide, refuses to apologise, and absolutely refuses to be anything other than unapologetically herself. She's the embodiment of freedom, but at a price: she's seen as immoral and repugnant, and is forever relegated to the margins of society.

But let's get real for a moment – why the heck does the size of breasts even come into play here? Well, it's all part of this weird, age-old narrative that says that women's bodies will tell you everything you need to know. It's a narrative that reduces women to a collection of body parts, each one attached to a very specific role. You're either the Madonna with your small, unassuming chest that says, 'Look, I'm pure and untouched', or the Whore with your large, loud breasts that scream, 'Sexual freedom and autonomy, baby!' We're so conditioned to this line of thinking that we can't even conceptualise a world where a woman could be both. Heaven forbid a woman with large breasts also have a deep, intellectual conversation about philosophy. Or a woman with small breasts could be sexually confident and empowered. That would throw everything off.

The Madonna–Whore division assumes that if you are sexually active, you're automatically a 'Whore'. But let's be honest for a second: what's so wrong with being a Whore? Is it so bad to want to own your sexuality, to embrace it, to be loud and unapologetic about it? Is it really that terrible to express yourself through your body, whether that's through the size of your breasts, the cut of your clothes or the way you move through the world? Does having big breasts or showing them off suddenly strip you of your humanity and dignity? Is it so bad to want to experience joy, fun and sexual freedom without being pegged as a 'Whore' just because you're not playing by society's restrictive rules?

On the flipside, the Madonna is painted as the epitome of virtue and respectability, but let's not forget that this narrative often comes with its own dark side. The expectation to be 'pure' and 'modest' can be just as suffocating. Women are constantly told they must fit a mould, to be a certain size, to behave a certain way, or risk being labelled as 'bad'. The Madonna is expected to repress her desires, to be a passive vessel of virtue. And while that might sound like a dream to some, the reality of living up to that expectation is stifling. No one can live their entire life trying to embody the Madonna while disregarding their own desires, needs and agency. It's exhausting.

Let's also take a moment to look at the historical context of this dichotomy. In everything from ancient Greek art to modern media, women have been objectified, idealised and reduced to their bodies, their looks and their ability to embody one of these roles. It's easy to look at a woman in a low-cut dress and assume she's a 'Whore', to dismiss her as one-dimensional, as if her body is all she is. It's easy to see a woman in a conservative outfit and assume she's a 'Madonna', as if her modesty somehow gives her more value. But in reality, both of these stereotypes are limiting and damaging. Women are so much more than the size of their breasts or how they choose to express their sexuality. Women are multifaceted beings with complex identities that can't and shouldn't be reduced to a binary of good or bad, pure or dirty.

So why does the Madonna–Whore Complex persist, through media, social media and the persistent policing of women's bodies? Perhaps it's because society finds it easier to control women by forcing them into neat little categories. Maybe it's because, deep down, we're uncomfortable with the idea of women who don't fit into our tidy little boxes. But the truth is, women have always existed in the grey area. Frankly, it's high time we stopped defining anyone as a Madonna or a Whore. We've always been more than just our breasts or our sexual history. We've always been complex, multifaceted and worthy of respect. And, at the end of the day, we're all just trying to figure out how to live our best, most authentic lives.

• • •

CHAPTER TWENTY

Saint Agatha of Sicily ... and her severed breasts

Saint Agatha of Sicily is a revered figure among Christian saints, particularly known for her extraordinary faith and the gruesome trials she endured during her martyrdom, some of which involve her breasts. Born around 231 AD in Sicily, Agatha came from a wealthy and noble family. From an early age, she dedicated herself to a life of chastity and piety, committing herself wholly to the Christian faith.

Agatha's beauty and virtue attracted the attention of Quintianus, the Roman prefect of Sicily, who desired her for his wife. Well ... here's trouble. When Agatha refused his advances and reaffirmed her vow of chastity, Quintianus subjected her to severe punishments, hoping to break her spirit and force her to renounce her faith. This period of intense persecution was during the reign of Emperor Decius, who decreed severe measures against Christians.

One of the most infamous tortures that Agatha endured was the mutilation of her breasts. Quintianus, in his fury and frustration at her steadfastness, ordered that her breasts be cut off. This brutal act was intended not only to physically torment her but also to degrade and humiliate her. Despite the excruciating pain, Agatha remained resolute in her faith. According to tradition, she was comforted by a vision of Saint Peter, who miraculously healed her wounds during the night.

Saint Agatha is often depicted holding her severed breasts on a platter, which has become a symbol of her martyrdom and suffering. This imagery is profoundly powerful, representing her unwavering faith and the brutality she endured.

Agatha's ordeal did not end with the mutilation of her breasts. She was further subjected to imprisonment, starvation and burning coals. Ultimately, she succumbed to her injuries and died in 251 AD. Her death, however, only solidified her sanctity in the eyes of the early Christian community. Agatha was venerated as a martyr almost immediately after her death, and her feast day is celebrated on 5 February each year.

Her harrowing ordeal also inspired an Italian dessert. Minne di Sant'Agata are small, breast-shaped pastries that are typically made from a rich, sweet dough filled with ricotta cheese, chocolate chips and sometimes candied fruit. The pastries are covered with a white icing or marzipan to represent skin and topped with a small piece of candied cherry to symbolise the severed nipple.

Question: do you reckon a venerated male Catholic saint whose penis was severed would have a penis-shaped pastry named after him?

• • •

CHAPTER TWENTY-ONE

The question of gender

Connor is 21 years old, a trans man living his life with a level of wisdom that would make anyone twice his age feel slightly inadequate. We first meet virtually – across the vast expanse of the internet, thanks to a Zoom call that's a touch awkward at first but quickly evolves into something entirely different. It's not just the usual 'getting to know you' chitchat; it's a conversation that feels grounded, profound and entirely unexpected. Sitting in some corner of Europe, taking a break from travelling, Connor has a calmness that makes me feel like I'm speaking with someone who's lived through decades of wisdom and hardship, when in reality he's a young man still figuring out how to navigate the complexities of life.

'I'm twenty-one,' Connor tells me, his words smooth and measured. 'But I feel like I've had plenty of professions. I've been a translator, a tutor, a drag queen, and now I work in retail. I've always had a passion for language and music. It all really comes down to communicating and connecting with people – understanding them. Even in retail, I feel like I'm helping people. When I speak to them in their own language, I can see the relief on their faces. That's when I know I'm doing something good.'

It's clear from the get-go that Connor is someone who's all about connection. He gets it – this deep, empathic understanding of the human experience. He's not someone who sees life as a series of roles to be played; he sees it as a journey of understanding and making a difference in the ways that matter most. And it's impossible not to feel moved by his words. There's a quiet passion behind them – a passion for human connection that transcends the mundane.

But as we dive deeper into the conversation, I begin to understand that Connor's journey is far more complex than just his work in retail or his various past professions. It's about the journey of self-discovery, acceptance and, ultimately, freedom. Freedom from the constraints of a body that never quite felt like his own.

Connor tells me about his experience with chest masculinisation surgery. His voice, steady and measured, takes on a new intensity as he recounts the details.

'In the lead-up to the surgery,' Connor explains, 'there were a lot of meetings – psychological evaluations, meetings with my psychiatrist, with my GP, with the surgeon. And I was nervous. My grandpa drove me to the hospital. He asked me, "Do you want me to stay?" but I said no. Inside, though, I was terrified. Terrified because I was going under anaesthesia, terrified because there's always that lingering question of whether you'll wake up and terrified because I had no idea what I would feel like after the surgery. I had seen other trans men who were overwhelmed and emotional after their surgeries, and I didn't know if I would react the same way. I'm not great with uncertainty. But when I woke up, all I felt was relief. A sense of freedom. It was like this weight had been lifted from me, and I felt like I was finally at home in my own body. It was an overwhelming sense of calm.'

His words strike a chord. It's the kind of calm that only comes after a long time living in a body that doesn't feel like yours. A calm that comes from feeling like you've finally been able to align your inner self with your outer appearance. And, in that moment, it becomes abundantly clear that Connor's journey is one of reclamation – not just of his body, but of his own sense of self.

'Before the surgery,' Connor continues, 'living in my body felt like a battle. Externally, everything would seem okay, but when I was alone, when I looked in the mirror, I felt so distressed. I've probably always felt like a stranger in my own body, but I didn't have the language to describe it at the time. It just felt wrong. I remember trying to figure out what was going on, trying to make sense of this feeling. I started trying to be hyper-feminine when I was in school – it was a sad attempt at fitting in. I overcompensated. I put on a bunch of weight, became depressed. I was like a stranger in my own body. I didn't fully realise what was happening until I was around thirteen or fourteen. Then I went through a period where I wore really baggy clothes to hide myself. To go unseen.'

The sadness in Connor's voice is palpable. It's the sadness that comes with not knowing how to articulate a feeling that runs deep inside you, a feeling that others might never understand because it doesn't have a name. But even through the sadness, there's this underlying resilience – a sense of determination. Connor was eventually able to push through the confusion, to embrace the truth of who he was, even when the world didn't yet recognise him for it.

'When I turned eighteen, I started on testosterone,' Connor tells me. 'Things started to change. It was a game changer. I went from having these full, nice breasts to just skin – skin and muscle. No fat, just muscle. Testosterone changes everything: your bone density, your hair follicles, your muscle structure, your voice. The voice change was the most significant thing for me. That was the moment I knew something real had shifted. I was so happy with the sound of my voice. It felt right. The only thing I wasn't thrilled about was the receding hairline,' he laughs.

I chuckle along with him. 'It's always something, right?' I say. There's always something about the body that we don't quite like, no matter how much we transform it.

'But I didn't feel like I was there yet,' Connor continues. 'I wanted the chest masculinisation surgery. And now that I've had it, I finally feel at ease. I feel like I'm mostly where I want to be. That said, I know I'll probably need to go through bottom surgery in my thirties or forties, but that's a huge procedure, and for now, I'm okay with where I'm at.'

I can hear the satisfaction in his voice. It's a satisfaction that comes not from the world's approval but from his own sense of alignment. Finally, after years of battling discomfort in his own skin, Connor has found a space in which he can simply exist, no longer fighting against himself.

'I'm experiencing summer in Europe right now,' he says, his voice lightening. 'I get to take my shirt off at the beach and feel comfortable. I used to hate the beach, but now? I just feel pure joy. You know, for trans people, transitioning takes up so much of your life. It takes up so much of your childhood. I feel like I can finally be young. Like I can finally experience being young without constantly worrying about how I look or how I feel.'

That is the essence of freedom, I think to myself. Freedom to simply exist. To be present in your body without fear, without shame. To live a life that doesn't feel like it's defined by an ongoing struggle for self-acceptance.

'One of the biggest changes for me,' Connor adds, 'is that I can have sex now. Before, I didn't have a sex life because I was so uncomfortable in my own skin. Now, I'm confident. I can be present with myself, with my body, and with someone else.'

There's a tenderness in his words, a softness that speaks to how deeply he understands the importance of being comfortable with oneself – not just in private but in intimacy. The liberation that comes with being able to exist fully in your body is something so many of us take for granted, and it's only when we hear stories like Connor's that we realise just how precious that liberation truly is.

'I had a lot of support getting here,' he continues. 'DJ Miss Victoria Anthony mentored me, and a lot of people in the drag scene helped me along the way. I'm so grateful for them. And to people who feel like I did when I was younger, I would say – it does get better. You just have to push through. Be patient, and make sure you have a solid support network. GPs, psychologists, psychiatrists. They make all the difference.'

His voice softens again. 'But what I would say is that transitioning isn't about a specific checklist. It's not necessarily a question of gender. There are trans men who don't go through chest masculinisation surgery and are perfectly happy. It's about what you're comfortable with. It's about how you express your gender, how you express your identity, your embodiment. For me, now, being in this body, it's pure joy. It's just pure joy.'

His words linger in the air, hanging there like a gift. A reminder that gender is a deeply personal journey, and that there is no single path to self-discovery. It's a reminder that, at the end of the day, we all deserve the joy of living in a body that feels like ours. A body that isn't a source of struggle but a place of peace. And for Connor, that peace is a reality. And I can't help but feel grateful to have shared even a fraction of that journey with him.

• • •

CHAPTER TWENTY-TWO

Empowerment? Or the pornification of women's bodies?

What's wrong with women adjusting their breasts to feel better about themselves, or to relieve chronic pain, or even for other medical reasons? As you'll later read, Dr Moradi describes how breast surgeons don't just work on breast augmentations but on all types of adjustments that aim to make life more liveable. And if we were to dwell on breast augmentations per se, can't they be viewed as empowering, a way for women to renegotiate their identities through their bodies, giving way to a different life?

There's a remarkable tension here – between empowerment on the one hand, and the patriarchal control of human bodies on the other. By this I mean men making decisions around women's bodies. We find ourselves stuck in a space between the emancipation of the female physique through modern surgery, and the sociopolitical meaning of the human body: the way bodies need to be policed and bound; a place where 'ugly' bodies (or those perceived to be ugly) are not allowed.

Are we simply being fed a rhetoric of choice around standards of beauty, while at the same time being steadily counselled and directed towards a set of supposedly 'appropriate' standards – via online commentary, social media and offline media? And, if so, is this surveillance and direction so powerful that there *is* no real choice?

Moulding to beauty standards

The idea of modifying the body to adhere to certain beauty standards is not new. Throughout history, standards of beauty have changed through time and culture. Ancient Egyptian women were expected to be round and golden in tone, while Queen Elizabeth I was seen as the epitome in beauty standards during the Elizabethan era, with her red hair and pale skin. However, the modern era has seen a significant shift, largely influenced by the proliferation of media and the pervasive reach of pornography.

Breast implants occupy a complex and multifaceted place within this discussion. Importantly, they are often linked to ideas about the pornification of women's bodies and 'raunch' culture. Introduced as a medical innovation, they were initially intended for breast reconstructions. Over time, implants became synonymous with cosmetic enhancement, closely tied to ideals of beauty perpetuated by media and pop culture.

The advent of the internet and the ensuing explosion of pornography into the mainstream cannot be understated in this context. Pornography, once a clandestine industry, has become omnipresent. Its influence permeates all forms of media, shaping perceptions of beauty and desirability.

In porn, exaggerated features such as large breasts and buttocks are often emphasised, creating a standard that has seeped into the consciousness of the general populace.

As a result, the line between empowerment and objectification becomes blurred. On one hand, breast implants can be argued to be a form of empowerment. Women have the autonomy to make decisions about their bodies, including undergoing cosmetic surgery to enhance their appearance. For many, breast implants can boost self-esteem, confidence and a sense of control over their body image. This perspective aligns with the broader feminist principle of bodily autonomy, asserting that women should have the freedom to choose what makes them feel most empowered.

However, this argument is complicated by the pervasive influence of the pornographic aesthetic in everyday life. The ubiquity of porn has transported its exaggerated standards of beauty into the ordinary world – from large breasts and bums to surgically enhanced lips, fake eyelashes, hair extensions and beyond.

Mainstream media, fashion and even social media platforms have adopted and normalised these ideals. Celebrities and influencers flaunt surgically enhanced bodies, reinforcing the notion that large breasts and buttocks are the pinnacle of attractiveness. Platforms like Instagram and TikTok, which are heavily visual, have become breeding grounds for the proliferation of the pornographic aesthetic. Influencers, often rewarded with likes and followers for their adherence to these beauty norms, perpetuate the cycle. The feedback loop created by social media can lead to a homogenised standard of beauty, where deviating from the norm is less acceptable.

This normalisation raises concerns about the extent to which these beauty standards are genuinely empowering or if they are, in fact, a manifestation of deeper societal pressures. The argument here is that the desire for breast implants might not stem solely from individual autonomy but from subconsciously adhering to a beauty ideal that is heavily influenced by pornographic imagery. The pressure to conform to these exaggerated standards can be overwhelming, particularly for young women who are bombarded with these images from a young age.

Moreover, the fetishisation of certain body parts – like breasts, for example – as popularised by porn, can reduce women to mere objects of sexual desire. This objectification undermines the very notion of empowerment. When women feel compelled to alter their bodies to meet an externally imposed standard, their autonomy is compromised. Instead of making a free choice, they may be responding to an ingrained belief that their value is tied to their physical appearance. But, like anything, there are always shades of grey. It may seem obvious, but our negotiations with our bodies do evolve over time. At one stage in life, we might adhere to a particular beauty ideal – whether in terms of body shape, breast size, makeup or hairstyle – but as we grow and our sense of identity shifts, we may find that those standards no longer resonate with us. In response, we adjust how we present ourselves, aligning with different ideals that better reflect who we are at that moment. This isn't a sign of inconsistency, as some might suggest, but rather a natural expression of identity and personal choice.

'Slim-thick'

This brings us to the current cultural moment, where big breasts and buttocks are not only considered attractive but have become normalised. The 'slim-thick' body type, characterised by a small waist, large hips and large breasts, epitomises this trend. While this body type has historical roots in various cultures, its contemporary resurgence is heavily tied to media representation and the influence of porn.

What are the implications for women who naturally do not fit this mould? The pressure to conform can lead to body dissatisfaction, low self-esteem and a host of mental health issues. Cosmetic surgery, including breast implants, becomes a tempting solution to these insecurities, but it is not without risks.

Second, there is the issue of accessibility and privilege. Not all women can afford breast implants or other cosmetic procedures. This creates a disparity where only those with the means can attain the culturally endorsed body ideal, further entrenching social inequalities. The commodification of beauty then becomes a marker of socioeconomic status, where physical appearance is not just about personal preference but also about access to resources.

The cultural shift towards accepting and normalising surgically enhanced bodies also reflects broader societal values. It signals a shift towards the commodification of the female body, meaning that physical appearance is increasingly viewed as a commodity that can be bought and sold. This commodification aligns with the ideals of capitalism, where everything, including beauty, has a price. In this context, breast implants are not just a medical procedure but a consumer product marketed to women as a pathway to desirability and success.

We also need to acknowledge the role of patriarchy in shaping beauty standards. The emphasis on large breasts and buttocks can be traced back to male-dominated media and the male gaze, which prioritises certain body parts over others. The pornification of the female body, therefore, can be seen as a continuation of patriarchal control, where women's bodies are moulded to fit male fantasies ... and where women come to desire these bodies as a baked-in patriarchy. And men who are fed a steady diet of sexualised, large-breasted and large-butted women via pornography come to recognise this physique as the strange embodiment of lust, power, sex, beauty dominance, control and violence. What does this mean in practice for the way they behave towards women? Towards heterosexual sex?

However, it is essential to recognise the agency of women who choose to get breast implants. For some, the decision is deeply personal and tied to their sense of identity and self-worth. These women may view the procedure as a reclaiming of their bodies, an act of defiance against natural limitations, or a means of achieving a desired aesthetic that makes them feel powerful.

A tension

The tension between empowerment and pornification is not easily resolved. It exists in a space where a woman's individual autonomy intersects with external pressures. Breast implants, as a symbol, embody this tension. They represent the desire for control and autonomy over one's body while simultaneously reflecting the pervasive influence of external beauty standards.

Ultimately, the conversation around breast implants and their place along this spectrum of 'empowerment versus pornification' is ongoing. While some women may find breast implants empowering, others may feel they are succumbing to an externally imposed ideal. The challenge lies in navigating these conflicting narratives and fostering a culture where diverse body types are celebrated, and our ability to make our own choices is genuinely respected.

As society continues to evolve, so too will perceptions of beauty and the choices women make about their bodies. The key is to ensure that these choices are made freely, without undue influence from pervasive and often unrealistic standards. Empowerment, in its truest form, comes from within, and the journey to that empowerment is unique for each woman. Whether through breast implants or other means, the goal should always be to support women's agency and celebrate their diverse expressions of beauty.

• • •

CHAPTER TWENTY-THREE

Huge mistake. *Huge.*

Amanda

If you're blonde and big boobed, you can get away with murder.

I casually mentioned this in passing to Lisa. She laughed but there was a curiosity and intrigue in her response.

'Really? Stop it. Do you think so? I'll be going to jail then ...' she joked, and lamented her small but sophisticated natural breasts.

'Think so?' I replied. 'I *know* so.'

I'd just had my fifth or sixth boob job. I think fifth. I know, right – it's as if I am collecting shoes, not silicone. But it had been a decade at least since my first op, my skin had well and truly stretched, and I was used to having big boobs.

This time I decided to go under the knife with Dr Pouria Moradi. He was a friend of a friend, and I thought, *Why not? Time for a change.* It was Dr Moradi who took me from 800cc to 1050cc, at my request, which is the largest you can go in Australia. I was well entrenched as Samantha X, my books (*Hooked* and *Back on Top*) were still flying off the shelves, I had an escort agency (Samantha X Angels), and I was a regular in the media. Big boobs were my brand.

So having *really* big boobs was a no-brainer. They were huge, so why not go *massive*?

I had to have my old implants removed due to safety issues with those particular silicone ones, although nothing had happened to me – no side effects or leakage. But it was best to be safe.

'And while you're at it, Doc, we may as well go bigger ...'

'Bigger?'

After some deep discussions and measuring in our many consultations, and a psychology test I had to pass – a new questionnaire to make sure you weren't body dysmorphic (not greedy) – I went bigger. A lot bigger. And, dare I say it, too big.

Even for me.

I woke up from surgery and felt the huge mounds on my chest. Holy shit. They were massive, swollen *mountains*. High on drugs, and with the pain of an additional procedure – a brand-new lower facelift – to recover from, I didn't think about my breasts much. It was only when the pain and swelling subsided, and I was back at home, that I had a good hard look at myself in the mirror.

They were ENORMOUS. Good? Bad? I wasn't sure yet. But they were heavy and uncomfortable. Was that just me getting used to them? I couldn't tell.

After a week or so at home, I decided to take the car to the local car wash. While I was waiting for it to be cleaned, I sat inside and read the paper, my chest bursting out of my singlet. It was the first time I'd left the house since my recovery – a litmus test, a trial run to test out the new additions.

'Amanda, hi! How are you? Fancy seeing you here!' a woman's voice interrupted me.

I looked up. It was Sarah and her partner Dan, a beautiful couple I knew from my local cafe. They'd recently got engaged.

'Oh, hi!' I smiled. 'How are you both?'

'Oh, just wonderful,' Sarah said. 'We're just planning our wedding. I've got the dress, Dan picked the venue, we're thinking about Fiji for our honeymoon ...'

'Can't wait,' murmured Dan, looking in his future wife's eyes lovingly.

And as they stood there making love with their eyes, I felt my own burn with salty hot tears. I forced a grin. 'How lovely,' I replied.

How lovely. How nice. How perfect she was, with her nice life, and her perfect body, and her perfect, small, sophisticated, natural, *marriage-material* boobs.

'And how have you been?' she asked sweetly. 'I hear

you've just had surgery. How are you feeling?' Her eyes gave a quick flick to my chest and then met my eyes again. She was probably wondering what the hell I had done to my body.

'Oh fine, yes, very happy,' I replied, swallowing a huge sob in my throat.

And it was there, sitting in the car wash, listening to Sarah and Dan telling me about the flowers, the honeymoon, the guests and the food, that I felt a heavy sadness overwhelm me.

I felt like a circus freak. I had designed my body to be undateable.

No one was ever going to date me, let alone marry me, with ridiculous big fake tits like mine! Not that I wanted to get married – I just wasn't that type. That nice-girl type, that kind of girl ... but what *was* I? I barely recognised myself in the mirror anymore. Had I gone too far?

'I'm a fucking joke. I am disgusting. My tits are way too big. What have I done to myself?' I wailed to my friend Madison on the phone as soon as I got home. 'They felt *sorry* for me. I look like a washed-up old slapper with big, stupid, fake tits.'

'Oh for god's sake, Amanda, you're coming down off the drugs. Most women would kill to be blonde with big fake tits. Stop wallowing.'

But that incident in the car wash was just the beginning. That was when the problems started – the angst, the realisation that actually, maybe, I'd tipped the scales a little too much.

And, as my anecdotes usually happen when I am out walking, so did this one. It was just after Covid, I had my huge boobs, and I went for a walk along the coastline. 'OMG look at that woman's boobs,' sniggered a young girl to her boyfriend, who laughed just as I walked past.

My face burned. How humiliating. I put my jumper on and once again cursed the fact I was so insecure. Why couldn't I be 'normal'? Why couldn't I just be one of those women who was happy the way God made her? What happened to Amanda Goff, socially acceptable journalist, nice girl, the girl men wanted to show off to their friends?

Now what was I – some laughing stock? A joke? The Jocelyn Wildenstein of Bondi?

It was a thought merely confirmed to me by someone I know – a female 'friend' who, when I told her of my dream to one day become a Pilates teacher, sneered and said, 'You? Ha ha! Who is going to come to your classes and take you seriously when you ... you look the way you do? Hardly empowering!'

She gave me the once-over, from head to toe and face to breasts – definitely the breasts – and laughed.

Wow, I thought. *I really do look that bad*. It wasn't just in my head.

I went home with two things on my mind: how much I hated myself, and a desire to rip the two fat silicone implants out of my disgusting fake body. *Oh, Amanda. What have you done?*

If it were that simple, of course, I would have booked the operation and been done with it.

But it wasn't simple. Nothing is.

• • •

CHAPTER TWENTY-FOUR

Dr Moradi

Amanda and I arrived at Dr Pouria Moradi's practice on Bourke Street in Surry Hills on an unseasonably cold summer's day, in the kind of chilly air that seemed more fitting for autumn. The building itself was striking – a former church, now gutted and repurposed into an expansive medical practice. I couldn't help but marvel at the massive stained-glass windows, the vestiges of the church's past that stood like grand, colourful sentinels in the midst of this very modern space.

I immediately felt a wave of nervousness. This wasn't the kind of world I usually found myself in. It wasn't just the building; it was the very nature of the practice. Plastic surgery, specifically breast augmentation, felt foreign, and I didn't quite understand the rules. Silicone, saline, teardrop, round – these were terms I knew only by name, and even then only vaguely. There was something taboo about entering a plastic surgeon's office, as if there were an unspoken judgement hanging in the air. After all, when you walk into a place like this, you're coming in to change something about yourself, to modify your body.

As I sat in the low-lying, emerald-velvet chair in the waiting room with Amanda, I found myself sneaking glances at the other patients. The first woman, slender and dressed in business attire, flicked through her phone absently, not an ounce of suggestiveness about her. She certainly didn't give off the vibe of an escort or a porn star. But the second woman, well, she was a different story. Large breasts, an exaggerated amount of cleavage and lips that looked like they had been inflated to near cartoonish proportions – she was flipping through her phone just as absently, but there was no mistaking the cues. The way she was dressed, the way she held herself, made me think she could easily be an escort or an OnlyFans star.

I mentally scolded myself for making such snap judgements. It's strange how the physical body comes with its own set of codes to read, a semiotic language that we all seem to unconsciously speak.

I turned to Amanda, needing to distract myself from my misplaced assumptions. 'I went to see a psychic the other day,' I said, trying to steer my thoughts elsewhere.

'Did you?' Amanda's interest was piqued immediately.

We were both women who liked to visit psychics – an odd, unspoken thing we both shared. I had been at a career crossroads for what felt like a lifetime, trudging through mindless communications jobs that paid the bills but drained my soul. It wasn't that I didn't enjoy the work, but it wasn't where my true passions lay. Writing, research, the things that made me feel alive, didn't bring in the kind of money that would cover rent, let alone anything else. I had been stuck in this endless cycle of juggling soul-crushing jobs while trying to keep my passion projects alive.

'Yes, in Newtown,' I continued, my thoughts momentarily drifting back to the psychic.

'And?' Amanda leaned in, clearly intrigued.

'Well, she said that things would just fall into place, that I wouldn't need to do anything drastic like resign. I just had to trust that it would happen on its own.'

'Right.' Amanda sounded unconvinced.

'Yeah, I know. She said to do nothing and not worry about it.'

'Nothing?' Amanda raised an eyebrow.

I sighed. 'I know we both struggle with doing nothing. We're the type of women who always need to be doing something – always forcing action, always trying to make something happen.'

Amanda and I were both 'doers' – the kind of women who couldn't let go of control, who couldn't just let things unfold. We always needed to see immediate results.

'We struggle ...' Amanda trailed off, her eyes wandering to the woman with the over-the-top breasts, her gaze snapping back to me quickly. 'See! Over there,' she whispered.

I gave her a noncommittal smile. 'Yes, I see.'

'Amanda?' Dr Moradi's voice interrupted our conversation, his presence immediately commanding the room.

Amanda jumped up. 'Hi, Doctor!' She waved enthusiastically, and we both followed her into his office.

Dr Moradi was a striking man – silver-haired, with a sharp jawline and an air of effortless confidence. His presence was immediately imposing, and his attire – a perfectly tailored suit, well-polished shoes and a sharp demeanour – spoke of a man who had his life together, down to the smallest detail. He didn't strike me as someone who ever let anything slip, and I could already tell he was a perfectionist in every sense of the word.

'Doctor, lovely to meet you,' I said, shaking his hand as we settled into seats around an oval table in his office.

'I have your book,' I said, waving a copy of Dr Moradi's book *Normal* in front of him, signalling my genuine interest.

'Fantastic. Thank you for your support,' he replied with a smile.

I had skimmed through the book, intrigued by the premise – Dr Moradi's letter to his daughter about body image. The opening anecdote, about his daughter trying on swimsuits with innocent joy, made me reflect on the innocence of childhood and the inevitable loss of that confidence as we grow older. The book touched on the pressure girls face as they enter adolescence, especially concerning body image – an issue I too had encountered, but in a more nuanced way, particularly with my own daughter. It made me think deeply about how much pressure we place on women's bodies, how we critique and judge them, often from an incredibly young age.

Dr Moradi's office was methodical, precise – everything in its place. He was the kind of man who lived by a strict routine. He didn't strike me as someone who had any vices. His diet was probably a regimented balance of protein and greens, his mornings well structured with exercise, and his evening routine carefully planned, winding down with eye creams and sleep aids. I, on the other hand, lived a life that felt more chaotic. My clothes always seemed to have some stain, I struggled to maintain routines, and I was prone to indulging in the occasional glass of champagne – and sometimes, too many. I envied his structure, his discipline.

'So,' he said, directing his attention to Amanda. 'Tell me about your upcoming surgery. What are you thinking?'

Amanda launched into a brief explanation, and I could tell Dr Moradi was already formulating a plan in his mind, his focus unwavering as he typed away on his keyboard.

'Well, I want to go smaller, but not too small. I still want big boobs,' Amanda said.

Dr Moradi turned to a chart of breast implants, showing different sizes and shapes. 'Currently, you have the 1050cc implants, the largest on the market,' he said. 'But these have been discontinued.'

Amanda seemed surprised, but she nodded.

'So, how much smaller are you thinking?'

'Seventy to fifty per cent of what they are now. As a friend of mine said, "I still want big boobs, just not hooker-sized boobs." I want "normal"-woman-sized boobs,' Amanda said, her British accent sharp as she spoke, as if this were a conversation she had all the time.

Dr Moradi nodded, analysing her request. 'Perhaps the 750cc in the same range? That would give you the same projection and width, but about twenty-five per cent smaller.'

The two of them spent the next few moments discussing measurements, projections and various implant options. To be honest, I had no idea what any of it meant, but I appreciated the way they spoke so comfortably about it. It was a world that felt foreign to me, but I found myself wanting to understand it more.

'I think this size will work,' Amanda said decisively, putting both hands on the implants to feel the difference.

I was amazed at how quickly she made her decision. Me? I would have spent hours considering every option, agonising over every detail. But then again, I hadn't done the research Amanda had.

After a few more moments of discussion, Dr Moradi moved onto the next phase of the consultation. He gestured toward Amanda. 'Let me take a look at where you're at,' he said.

Amanda jumped to her feet, and the two of them moved into the next room. I stayed behind, flipping through the 'breast book' on the table in front of me, hoping to glean something useful for my own research.

When they returned, Dr Moradi turned his attention to me. I gave him a brief overview of the book I was working on and asked him some opening questions about his career and the surgeries he performs. He told me he had been a surgeon for twenty years, specialising in breast, tummy and facial surgeries. He noted that combination surgeries were common – often breast and tummy, or breast and rhinoplasty.

'So, do you think the trend in implants has changed over time? Are women going bigger or smaller?' I asked.

Dr Moradi paused before answering. 'There's definitely a trend for smaller breasts at the moment. A lot of women are opting for smaller implants these days, sometimes as small as 180cc. It's becoming more common.'

Amanda seemed surprised. From the chart, I could see that 180cc was the smallest option.

'Why is that?' I asked.

'Social media plays a big role,' he explained. 'Celebrities and influencers have a huge impact on what women want. The Pamela Anderson days are over,' he added with a chuckle.

I nodded, intrigued. 'Do you think there's a certain type of woman who gets breast augmentations?'

Dr Moradi's response was quick. 'No, absolutely not. There are all sorts of women who come in for surgery. Some want a breast reduction because of back pain, while others are post-pregnancy and want to restore what they had before. It's all about personal choice.'

His response made sense. Women came in for a variety of reasons, and the choice was highly individual.

We continued to discuss trends in the industry, mental health and how the pressure to conform to beauty standards played a role in the decision to undergo surgery. As our time came to a close, I couldn't help but feel like I had only scratched the surface of this complex world.

As we left his office, Amanda turned to me. 'So, did you like him?'

'Yeah, nice guy,' I said. 'He seems capable of navigating this complex environment.'

'So, are you going to get yours done?' she asked, her tone sly.

I paused for a moment. 'I don't know,' I said. 'The more I learn about it, the more I think ... maybe not.'

• • •

CHAPTER TWENTY-FIVE

Seventy-two pairs of breasts

My friend and I attended an art exhibition. We had been art pals since our schooldays – nobody else we knew was the least bit interested in such things. This time, we'd just visited an exhibit showcasing the works of Pablo Picasso and Henri Matisse, and let me tell you: it was a lot of breasts. Seventy-two pairs, to be exact. That's not a typo. Seventy. Two.

As we navigated the gallery, my initial reaction was to marvel at the artistry – the sharp angles of Matisse's nudes, the surreal layers of Picasso's cubist forms. But soon, a growing sense of unease began to creep in. Did these men love breasts, or did they love the power to display them, reduce them, manipulate them? Were they celebrating the female form, or merely objectifying it under the guise of art?

'Picasso, at least, didn't bother hiding his misogyny,' my friend said, gesturing at a sketch titled *Minotaure caressant une dormeuse*. In it, a young woman – modelled on Picasso's lover Marie-Thérèse Walter – lies asleep, being groped by a minotaur.

The minotaur is Picasso, of course, because why wouldn't he self-portrait as a man/bull sexually assaulting his muse? Insert eye roll here. This wasn't just art; it was autobiography.

Picasso's granddaughter Marina described his treatment of women as a process of 'extracting their essence'. Then, she wrote, 'once they were bled dry, he would dispose of them'. Indeed, two of his female muses – including Marie-Thérèse – committed suicide. And yet there we were, walking through a gallery that seemed to glorify the man. I wondered how many other visitors had stopped to consider the ethical implications of ogling a sculpted pair of breasts created by a man who openly treated women as consumable.

Matisse's work was slightly easier to digest, but only marginally. His 'odalisques' – richly coloured, dreamlike portraits of concubines – are beautiful, yes, but they come with their own baggage. These paintings aren't just about the female form; they're steeped in Orientalism, a movement that romanticised and eroticised the 'exotic' East for the pleasure of Western audiences. Matisse's women, draped in silks and adorned with beaded anklets, were fantasies, not individuals. Their beauty existed solely for the gaze of a white, male viewer.

I stood in front of *Odalisque à la culotte grise*, a painting of a reclining woman in grey-green harem pants, her deep red nipples a stark contrast to her milky-pink skin. 'It's stunning,' I said, almost guiltily. 'But it's also ... gross?'

'Exactly,' my friend replied. 'It's like eating a delicious meal and then realising it's made of stolen ingredients. You want to enjoy it, but you also want to yell at the chef.'

She had a point. The art was breathtaking, but its

implications were troubling. These women were reduced to ornaments – beautiful, yes, but passive and powerless. Matisse capitalised on their femininity and ethnicity, crafting works that were as much about Western colonial fantasies as they were about artistic skill.

If artists like Picasso and Matisse are no longer alive to answer for their work, the responsibility shifts to the galleries that display them. Context matters. A painting of a nude isn't inherently problematic, but when it's paired with an artist's history of misogyny or a movement like Orientalism, it demands explanation.

'Imagine if, next to every odalisque, there was a placard explaining Orientalism,' I mused aloud. 'Like, "Hey, just so you know, these paintings perpetuate harmful stereotypes and were part of a broader colonial narrative."'

'That's the dream,' my friend said. 'But galleries don't want to scare off donors by being too "political".'

'Which is hilarious,' I added, 'because what's more political than art?'

Still, not all depictions of the female form are problematic. Artists like Australia's Prudence Flint and Kim Leutwyler offer a refreshing counterpoint. Flint's intimate portrayals of women brushing their teeth or breastfeeding capture the mundane beauty of everyday life. Leutwyler's vibrant portraits of queer women celebrate their identities rather than reducing them to objects of desire. These works are about empowerment, not objectification.

The difference lies in intention. Picasso's nudes were about conquest; Flint's are about connection. Matisse's odalisques catered to male fantasies; Leutwyler's paintings amplify queer voices. When art respects its subjects, it elevates them. When it doesn't, it risks perpetuating the very inequalities we're trying to dismantle.

'Maybe that's the real issue,' my friend said as we left the gallery. 'It's not that Picasso and Matisse painted breasts. It's that they painted breasts without asking what the breasts wanted.'

I laughed. 'What do breasts want? Freedom? Representation? Less fried-egg symbolism in fashion?'

'All of the above,' she replied, grinning.

Later that evening, as we sipped wine and scrolled through Instagram, I came across Leutwyler's work. One painting, in particular, stood out: a bold, unapologetic portrait of a woman with her chest bare, her gaze steady and self-assured. It was the antithesis of the current exhibit – less about the breasts themselves and more about the person they belonged to.

'Now *this* is empowering,' I said, showing my friend the image.

She nodded. 'See? It's not about covering up or baring all. It's about the context. Who's painting, why they're painting and who gets to decide what it all means.'

It's not about erasing Picasso and Matisse from history; it's about presenting their art with honesty. Acknowledge the brilliance, yes, but also the flaws. Art doesn't exist in a vacuum, and neither should its critique.

But for fuck's sake, it was all so deeply complex!

'Don't get me started on Gauguin,' my friend said and sighed.

• • •

CHAPTER TWENTY-SIX

You remind me of my favourite porn star

It's a Monday morning and I'm in the thick of navigating heavy traffic to work when I get a call from Amanda.

'Well, hello!' I coo, tapping the button on my steering wheel to activate the hands-free.

'Doctor Love, how are you?' she quips.

'I'm well – in traffic.'

'I have a dating app anecdote for your research,' she dives in.

'Please, break up the monotony of this drive for me.'

'So firstly, I'm on Bumble last night chatting to this guy: late thirties, office-worker type. Seems nice enough – gentlemanly, even. Anyhoo, as the evening progresses, and perhaps he's had a couple of drinks at this stage, he messages me: *You remind me of my favourite porn star*.'

'He did *not*!' I say, shocked, as I always am with these types of anecdotes.

'Yes! Don't sound so shocked – this isn't the first time I've heard this line. And they say it like it's supposed to be some sort of compliment.'

'Wow ... who are these people?'

'Men, that's who they are. So, I always try to catch them out when they say this ... Provocatively, I ask, "Who do you mean?" Because obviously, there's no *one* porn star for them – they just meld into one gigantic heap of big-breasted women. Of course he couldn't answer, but he made some reference to my boobs.'

'Oh lord ...'

'Exactly. Then, I said to him that I was actually having my breasts reduced shortly.'

'And?'

'He unmatched me.'

'He did *not*!'

'He did – he unmatched me. Yes, he mentioned something about surgery being body violation beforehand, but he didn't raise that in relation to my previous boob jobs.'

'The online world never ceases to amaze me,' I say, shaking my head. Of course, the online space was simply a reflection of the offline world, but something about the anonymity of the digital domain gave the depraved an extra edge or agenda.

'Hmmm ... I know. Okay, heading into Pilates, talk to you later.'

• • •

CHAPTER TWENTY-SEVEN

The Wonderbra

It was 1998, and I was in the thick of my 'Kate Moss is the future' phase. You know the one. I wore flannel shirts over ripped jeans, listened to Oasis on repeat and thought it was cool that I had a flat chest. I wasn't complaining. Who needed breasts when Kate Moss existed? She was flat-chested, too, and she was the poster child for cool in a way no one in the Sutherland Shire could even begin to grasp.

I had a friend named Kelly, who wasn't quite as cool as me. She was still in the business of trying to look like Cindy Crawford, which, at the time, felt like a lost cause. She had curves. Real ones. Not the ones you pretend you have when you wear a baggy T-shirt and a pair of baggy jeans like I did. Kelly, on the other hand, wore low-rise skirts and spaghetti-strap tops to showcase what could only be described as 'assets' that I had zero use for.

One day, Kelly popped over to my house, armed with a newspaper clipping she'd cut out from one of those trashy gossip mags.

'Lisa, you need to come with me to the shops,' she said dramatically, waving the page at me like it held the key to the universe. 'They have these things, and they're, like, a miracle. They make you look like you actually have something!'

'Something? What are we talking about here? A boob job?' I asked, flicking through my issue of *Dolly* magazine, trying to ignore the fact that my bra kept shifting up my back.

'No, not a boob job,' she said, raising an eyebrow as if I'd said something totally ridiculous. 'A Wonderbra, duh. You know, like, they make your boobs look ... well, amazing.'

I stopped flipping through my magazine and gave her my full attention. The Wonderbra. I had heard of it, of course. What kind of person would I have been if I hadn't? But to me, the whole idea seemed a bit ... well, *unnecessary*.

'Why would I need one of those?' I asked, eyeing her with suspicion. 'I'm happy with my ... whatever it is that I've got going on. Plus, isn't it a bit ... you know, fake?'

'Fake? It's just *enhancement*, Lisa!' Kelly said, clutching the clipping even more tightly. 'Don't you want to be one of those girls who can wear a strapless top and not feel like a kid playing dress-up?'

Hmmmm ... a disturbing comparison. I didn't want to feel like I was stuck in some sort of pre-adolescent stage of development while everyone else was turning heads at parties.

'Okay, let's say I do this. What if I just end up looking like one of those ... bimbo girls who hang out in Bondi?'

It was a different time.

Kelly snorted and gave me a withering look. 'Please. No one is going to think you're a Bondi bimbo. You'll just look ... better. Trust me.'

'Fine,' I said, rolling my eyes. 'Let's go. But you owe me if this goes wrong. I'm blaming you if I turn into some desperate attempt at a cleavage queen. You could be creating a monster.'

She rolled her eyes. 'I wish,' she murmured under her breath.

My feminist rhetoric wasn't exactly du jour some twenty-plus years ago in the Shire – I can tell you that much!

We hopped into her little red car, me clutching my *Dolly* magazine like it was a life raft, and Kelly's hands were firmly gripped on the wheel, her face set in a look of intense determination. We were on a mission. A mission to change my flat-chested future.

We pulled up to the mall, Miranda to be exact. We still called it Miranda Fair, even though it had been Miranda Westfield since the early '70s ... and it was all kinds of uncool. As we walked in, Kelly led the way like she was a seasoned Wonderbra shopper, which – let's be real – she probably was. I was in awe of how confident she was in her own body, with her ample chest jutting out and her curly hair bouncing as if she had every right to wear anything she damn well pleased.

The lingerie section was my personal version of hell. It was like a minefield of lacy things and uncomfortable-looking straps that seemed more for decoration than actual function. I had no clue what I was looking for, but Kelly was determined to turn me into some kind of '90s superwoman with cleavage that could break glass.

'There it is!' she cried, grabbing a box off the shelf and

practically shoving it into my hands.

I looked at the box, which was adorned with glossy images of women who looked like they might actually be able to support entire ecosystems with the size of their chests. 'Uh ... are you sure this is for me?' I asked. 'I mean, look at these women. They're practically walking on their own two massive breasts.'

'Trust me,' Kelly said, tossing it in my hands. 'Just try it on.'

So I found myself in a change room, staring at a fluorescent-lit mirror with a bra that seemed to promise me the world. I was sceptical. Very sceptical. This whole thing was ridiculous, right? After all, I didn't need a Wonderbra. I was a proud member of the flat-chest club. What did I have to prove?

But I put it on. And when I stepped out of the fitting room, Kelly's jaw dropped.

'Lisa,' she said slowly, as if she'd never seen me before. 'What have you done to yourself?'

I looked at her in the mirror. I was still me, but ... I looked like I actually had curves. Subtle curves, but curves nonetheless. I could almost feel the weight of them.

'Oh my god,' I said, my voice rising. 'I think I have ... *boobs*.' I grabbed them in mock horror. She didn't appreciate my antics.

Kelly slapped her hand to her forehead. 'You're not getting it, are you? You're not just *boobs*. You're a new woman. This is a *lifestyle*. You're going to be walking down the street like—'

'Like a supermodel?' I said, cutting her off.

'Exactly!' Kelly said, her eyes lighting up.

I rolled my eyes.

'I look ... ridiculous.' I mimicked a vomiting action at the same time. 'You've bought into this supermodel rhetoric,' I said, ignoring the fact that Kate Moss, my own idol, was also a supermodel. But, FYI, a *cool* one.

'What?' she said, shocked.

'Yeah. This is the dumbest thing I've ever seen. It will never take off.'

'It already has!' she hissed at me, pulling the curtain closed on the dressing room vehemently.

I shrugged.

• • •

CHAPTER TWENTY-EIGHT

As long as you're not getting them done to meet someone else

'I've been thinking of getting my breasts done,' I casually announced to my partner one nondescript Saturday night. You know, the kind of night where nothing exciting happens, and the most thrilling event is a slightly colder cup of tea than usual.

He looked at me with a face that said *I have no idea how I ended up in this conversation, and I wish I could go back in time to avoid it*. You know that face – men make it when anything involving women's bodies gets discussed. It's as if they've been handed a live grenade, and the pin has just been pulled. They know if they say the wrong thing, they will be trapped in a minefield of regret, their words echoing in the future like haunted ghosts. And let's be honest: they know their words will definitely be used against them in a trial years down the road.

'Why's that?' he asked cautiously, like he was walking through a field of landmines and didn't know which one would blow up first.

'Well, you know, when I was younger, I had that whole thin, flat-chested thing going on. And it was cute. They used to just ... sit there. All perky and pleased with themselves. Like two little happy buttons, you know?' I said, curling up on the couch beside him, tea in hand. My tone was almost wistful, like I was reminiscing about my childhood pet turtle or the good old days when my metabolism didn't need a pep talk.

He looked at me, sweat starting to bead on his forehead as he clearly realised the conversation was heading into dangerous waters.

'They still look cute,' he offered weakly. His words weren't even an attempt to comfort; they were a survival tactic. 'Cute' was his diplomatic escape route. I could practically hear his internal dialogue: *Say something safe. Don't screw this up. She's already looking at me like I've committed a war crime.*

'They don't,' I said, taking a sip of tea. 'After breastfeeding two babies, they're kind of ... sad. Depleted. Like a pair of old bells, just sort of hanging there.'

He blinked, probably trying to decide whether to keep digging or pretend he didn't hear that last bit. 'Well, I wouldn't go that far ...' he managed. I could see he was already exhausted by my internal monologue, which had turned into a full-blown analysis of my post-maternal cleavage. And truthfully, it was exhausting for me too. I didn't even know how we got here. One minute I was enjoying a cup of tea, and the next we were diving headfirst into my existential crisis over my breasts.

'It's true,' I insisted.

'Well, we're older now. That's what happens to bodies. They sag. They droop. It's unrealistic to think we're going to look like twenty-one-year-olds forever,' he said, probably hoping this statement would defuse the situation. Like he was the voice of reason in an otherwise chaotic universe.

'Ah yes,' I said, suddenly sounding a little more cynical. 'Enter the wonderful world of contemporary beauty standards, where sixty-year-old women are still expected to have silky-smooth skin and perky breasts. It's totally realistic to think we should all just freeze in time, right?'

I said it with such sarcasm that he winced. I could practically see the gears turning in his head as he tried to figure out how to back out of this conversation without being dismembered.

'I know,' I continued, because why stop when you've already made your partner feel like he's about to be dragged into a social justice documentary. 'I just don't feel comfortable with them anymore.'

Had all this self-reflection been brought on by endless online debates about breast augmentation, or was it deeper than that? Had I secretly always thought my breasts were unsatisfactory, but only now had the courage to face the truth? It was hard to say. I mean, I'd never really felt *bad* about my chest, but was there a sense of ... dissatisfaction? Probably.

He sighed, realising that the decision was entirely up to me, and there was no easy way out. 'It's up to you,' he said. 'If you want to do it, I won't object.' And I'm sure he was thinking, *But if you do it, I'll be mentally preparing for every single man on the planet to be commenting on your chest from now until the end of time.* But he didn't say that part out loud. Men are good at that – remaining silent while actively spiralling internally.

'Hmmm ...' I pondered aloud, pretending I needed more time to think, though in reality, I was already planning the whole procedure in my head.

'How much do these things cost?' Ah, the inevitable question. Finance – the great conversation killer.

'I think around $10,000 if you go with a not-so-expensive surgeon,' I said, almost casually, like that was pocket change. Like I wasn't also mentally calculating how many weeks of takeaway I'd have to sacrifice to make this happen.

He sighed deeply, his face betraying a little bit of panic, as though this conversation was spinning out of control and he wasn't sure how to reel it back in. 'It's up to you. It'll change your look, I suppose,' he said, but the unease in his voice was unmistakable.

'What do you mean?' I asked, half-smirking, fully aware of where this was going. I'd seen this scenario play out before in countless sitcoms, but I had a feeling mine would end with far more awkwardness.

His eyes widened. The quicksand was rising, and I was ready to watch him flounder.

'The thin, boyish type,' he said, the words almost tumbling out like they were part of a script he didn't entirely understand. He immediately regretted them, his face turning three shades of crimson.

'I wouldn't say *boyish*,' he added quickly, desperately trying to backtrack. 'I mean, you know, *curve-less*.'

I raised an eyebrow, fighting the urge to laugh. 'Boyish? Really? Now I feel like I should get a shirt that says "Boyish" on it just to match your description.'

'No, no, that's not what I meant,' he said, clearly digging himself deeper with every word. 'I just ... I don't mind, babe. As long as you're not getting them done to meet someone else.'

I froze. That's when I rolled my eyes so dramatically that I think I heard them click. Here we go.

'What?' he asked, sensing my shift in mood.

'Well, now you're implying that I want big boobs to snag some guy. Like that's the *key* to catching a man. Really?' I raised both eyebrows and stared him down.

He blinked, looking back at me with the kind of blank stare that only a man who has just made an egregious error can muster. And in that moment, it was clear: this conversation was over. I had him exactly where I wanted him.

'Well, I mean ...' he stammered, completely lost. 'That's, uh ... not what I meant. I just meant that, like ... um ...' He trailed off, searching for a lifeline that wasn't there.

'I know what you meant,' I said, putting the finishing touches on my point. 'You think that women get breast implants to impress men. Because apparently, that's the only reason we do anything with our bodies, right?'

He stared at me, the blankness still there, as if I had just shattered every myth he had about the female psyche.

Exhausting, I thought. *Just exhausting.*

• • •

CHAPTER TWENTY-NINE

A history of breast augmentations

Breast augmentation, which began as an odd mix of curiosity, necessity and a little bit of 'Let's see if this works', has a history that reads like a bizarre, trial-and-error science-fiction plot – minus the aliens and laser beams. The earliest attempts at augmenting breasts date back to the 19th century, in the shadowy corridors of surgery where things were more about 'What if this works?' than 'Does this sound like a good idea?'

In 1895, a surgeon in Germany named Vincenz Czerny made what many people now refer to as the first documented breast augmentation. He wasn't thinking about voluptuous silhouettes or Chanel adverts. Oh no, his motivation was much more noble and far less glamorous. Czerny used a patient's own fat tissue (from a benign tumour) to repair a breast after it had been disfigured due to cancer surgery. Yes, you heard that right: fat from a tumour was used to repair a breast. It's like telling someone that instead of throwing out a half-finished pizza, you used the leftovers to create a masterpiece. We're talking about raw, rudimentary experimentation, and yet it paved the way for future developments in the field.

But let's get this straight – no one at that point was out there going, 'Hey, you know what would make me feel better about my body? Some artificial enhancements to my chest.' That wouldn't come until much later, after multiple failed attempts at stuffing some pretty weird materials into women's bodies.

So, let's fast-forward to the 20th century, where things really started to take a dramatic (and often dangerous) turn. You see, in the early 1900s, some surgeons were a little more experimental than others. And when I say experimental, I mean trying to use things like paraffin wax, ivory, glass balls and even ox cartilage as breast implants. You know, standard materials you might find in a high-school science lab – or the bottom of a bargain bin at a weird antiques store. So, let's break this down ...

- Paraffin injections? Check. This technique led to severe inflammation, infection and the formation of hard lumps. But hey, if you didn't mind looking like a living art installation, it was a real conversation starter.
- Ivory and glass balls? Definitely not the 'natural' look we're all chasing today. This kind of augmentation made your chest look like someone had randomly shoved a bunch of objects into your body without asking if you wanted them there.
- Ox cartilage? Well, that's one way to guarantee that you'll always be the most interesting person at a dinner party, though no one will ever be able to figure out what exactly is going on with your chest.

The fact that these methods existed is both horrifying and hilarious in hindsight. It's like a toddler trying to build a spaceship with chewing gum and paper clips and declaring it ready for launch. Unsurprisingly, these early experiments didn't end well. There were lumps, infections, inflammation and all sorts of complications that surgeons probably didn't list in their brochures. Still, these days were a necessary stepping stone to what was about to come next. And what came next?

Silicone. Oh, yes.

In the mid-1960s, two plastic surgeons, Thomas Cronin and Frank Gerow, along with a little help from the Dow Corning Corporation, gave the world something that would forever change the landscape of chest enhancement: silicone breast implants. This was the holy grail of boobery, the next-level technology that promised to look and feel like real breasts – minus the unexpected lumps of ivory and paraffin. The first silicone augmentation surgery, performed in 1962 on Timmie Jean Lindsey (a Texan woman with a remarkably non-Texan name, but that's beside the point), was deemed a resounding success. Timmie Jean went on to rave about her new, more 'natural' bust, and the world couldn't stop talking about the miracle of silicone implants.

Fast-forward to the 1980s and 1990s, and silicone implants were the new black – until they weren't. Yes, these implants, which once seemed like the most innovative thing since sliced bread, began to cause some serious concern. Word got out that silicone implants could rupture or leak, possibly triggering autoimmune diseases or systemic health problems. The media, as it often does, whipped up a frenzy, and the US Food and Drug Administration stepped in, imposing a moratorium on silicone-filled breast implants in 1992. Suddenly, those silicone beauties were no longer the go-to option. The beauty world went into a frenzy of 'What do we do now?' And what did they do? They turned to saline-filled implants.

Now, saline implants weren't the most exciting of options. Sure, they didn't leak or rupture into a potentially toxic mess of silicone goo. But they also had a more, shall we say, *distinctive* feel. Imagine a water balloon but with a silicone shell. It's not the most natural sensation, but hey, it was safer, and that's what mattered. Saline implants were like the low-fat version of silicone implants – they might not have been as thrilling, but they got the job done without causing too many problems.

However, many patients still weren't thrilled with the feel of saline implants. They weren't exactly walking around with the soft, bouncy, Jennifer Aniston–approved chests of their dreams. Silicone, though, still had a special place in the heart of the enhancement industry. After all, if you weren't worried about the occasional leak (and, let's face it, who isn't?), silicone implants had a texture and flexibility that saline could never compete with. The debate raged on.

And then came the 2000s. Enter the era of gummy-bear implants. Yes, you heard me right – *gummy-bear* implants. And no, these were not actual gummy bears shoved into your chest (though, with the state of '90s innovation, it's possible someone tried it). These were actually cohesive gel implants, made with a silicone gel that held its shape much better than the earlier, more liquid-filled versions. The idea was that even if the implant shell ruptured, the gel would stay in place, preventing it from leaking all over the body like a poorly sealed yoghurt pouch.

By the early 2000s, breast augmentation had fully evolved into the highly advanced procedure we know today. Surgeons had fine-tuned their skills, and patients had become increasingly picky about their results. You could now choose implants that were more suited to your body type, preferences and lifestyle, which, let's be real, meant that people started expecting their breast enhancements to work in conjunction with their social media profiles. Natural-looking augmentation, in which surgeons aimed for a subtle lift or volume boost, became all the rage. Nobody wanted to walk around looking like a cartoon character anymore. Everyone wanted to be the 'just had a great workout' version of themselves – without actually having to work out, of course.

These days, breast augmentation isn't just a procedure; it's part of a lifestyle. Women are choosing more personalised approaches to their implants, using advanced technology to determine the right size, shape and placement for their new breasts. You can now consult with your surgeon about your body type, your expectations and your aesthetic goals before they even touch a scalpel. And let's not forget the role that social media plays in the process – if you can't share a before-and-after picture of your new chest, did you even go through the procedure?

In Australia, breast augmentation is one of the most popular cosmetic surgeries, with approximately 20,000 procedures performed annually. This is a significant increase over the past decade, fuelled by social acceptance, celebrity culture and the fact that the whole thing has been turned into a relatively routine procedure with minimal downtime. Australia is a big spender on cosmetic surgery, alongside countries like the US and Brazil. It's not just about augmenting breasts anymore – it's a multi-billion-dollar industry that includes everything from Botox to liposuction, and everyone's getting in on the action.

Back in the 1990s, the rise of breast augmentation reflected larger cultural shifts toward body modification. Now, it's all about self-expression, and if you feel like your self-expression requires a little more volume up top, well, who are we to judge? After all, everyone's just trying to live their best life – one implant at a time.

But let's not forget, regardless of all the new technology and trends, breast augmentation started with a humble attempt at repairing a woman's body after a medical procedure. It's funny to think about how far we've come from paraffin injections and ivory implants to the highly sophisticated, personalised options we have today. In the end, no matter how we augment our bodies, one thing is clear: we've come a long way since 1895, and the future of breast augmentation is still evolving.

• • •

CHAPTER THIRTY

Susan's story

While I have been a flat-chested person all my life, my friend Susan has had the exact opposite problem. Here she describes her experience as someone born with large breasts.

My nine-year-old granddaughter has just bounced into my sitting room. 'I've got something to show you,' she says. She pulls up her crop top to proudly exhibit the two tiny bumps on her chest. 'Look,' she says, 'I've got boobs!' She's clearly very excited about developing into a woman. 'I'm a tween,' she tells me, 'and soon I'll be a teenager!'

I remember finding similar bumps on my chest when I was about her age. It was a very different time. In the '50s, the moniker 'teenagers' had only just been invented and the concept of tweens didn't exist. As a child I hadn't seen my mother undressed, although I knew she'd breastfed my younger sisters with a towelling nappy thrown strategically over her shoulder. Breasts were not something we talked about. We would have both found the subject very embarrassing.

My first experience of a man noticing my tiny breasts was frightening. It was the summer before we emigrated from England to Australia. We lived in Surrey, a leafy county south of London. Walking distance from our house was a heath where my twin brother and I used to play Robin Hood and marbles. When it was warm enough, we pretended to swim, one foot on the bottom, in a pond within the heathlands.

On the day concerned, I was alone at the pond. It was getting late and I needed to go home. My swimsuit was wet and uncomfortable. I pulled it off and decided to walk home in just my shorts. What happened next has stayed with me for more than 65 years. A man of about my father's age appeared out of nowhere and began to fiddle with his trousers. At nine I didn't understand what he was doing but I knew it was wrong. I looked around for a place to escape and saw a tree. I was very quickly in its highest fork. I didn't look down. I just concentrated on counting leaves. Don't ask me why. Intuitively I must have known I needed to distract myself and to stay up the tree for as long as possible. Eventually, I ran out of leaves and realised I'd be late home for tea. I climbed down, keeping my eyes peeled for the man, but he seemed to have disappeared. I ran all the way home and didn't mention the experience to anyone. Children often feel guilty even when they're not.

Within a few months we'd arrived in Australia and were staying with a family in the Tasmanian bush while my father looked for work and somewhere for us to live. The children of the family ranged in age from seven to 23. I hung out with my brother and two of the boys of the family aged ten and 11. I remember being very popular when we played doctors in the attic of the old farmhouse. The boys were constantly examining me with improvised medical equipment and there was no doubt I enjoyed my newfound popularity. It seemed that playing with a girl wasn't 'sissy' if you were playing doctors. My brother looked uncomfortable during these games but because he needed the boys for friends he just went along with it.

Eventually, we moved to our new house. My embryonic breasts continued to grow. One night, when I was about 11, I overheard my parents talking and I knew the subject was me. 'You can't let her walk around like that,' said my father, referring to my unfettered breasts. 'She's a full-blown woman!' Within a few minutes my mother's arm appeared around my bedroom door holding a bra. 'Put that on,' she said. 'Don't come out until you have.' I struggled into the bra, which didn't fit me properly. My mother and I never discussed the matter again. She was clearly embarrassed by my physical development and, consequently, so was I.

By high school, my breasts had become much larger than my mother's. She was a nice neat 12B. By the time I was 12 I was at least a D cup. The only bras I owned were hand-me-downs of my mother's. I bulged out of them. During sport we were forced, both boys and girls, to run around the school oval. The boys always called out 'Big tits!' as my breasts bounced up and down. My biggest nightmare was the school doctor. In those days a doctor would visit schools once or twice a year. We'd have to strip down to our underwear to be examined. The other girls had small perky breasts in pretty trainer bras, while I was strapped into my mother's old, worn bras that didn't fit. It was humiliating.

Eventually I left school and earned my own money. For

the first time I was able to buy new underwear. I remember trying on bras in Myer. My first new bra was a lacy affair in black. I felt so glamorous wearing it although no one saw it but me and, later, my first boyfriend. The bra didn't fit, as the largest size available was only a D cup, but it was the best that I could buy at the time. I continued to keep myself supplied with the prettiest underwear I could afford.

Later I left home for Sydney. Fast-forward a few years and in 1971 I gave birth to my first and only child. I had been overweight before I fell pregnant but due to persistent morning sickness, I lost a lot of weight. The problem was that my breasts, which had swollen to an enormous size during the pregnancy, shrank to a fraction of that size very quickly after the birth. Consequently, I now had a wrinkled cleavage – not something you want in your twenties. I decided I needed to have breast surgery, not only to get rid of the wrinkled skin but to get rid of my oversized breasts once and for all. I wanted to look 'normal'. I wanted to be a 12B like my mother.

The operation took place in a Sydney hospital. Before the op I was told to buy two cotton bras in the size I had nominated as being my ideal. I enjoyed buying them. I was going to be normal at last. It was the '70s and flat chests were in fashion. Some women even went without bras. I didn't need to be flat exactly, but I didn't want to look like some '50s bombshell bursting out of my bras.

I was sooooo disappointed to wake up from the anaesthetic and find that I wasn't the 12B I'd requested. I was told the 'swelling' would go down, but I knew the nurses were lying. The male surgeon had decided that all I needed was to have my breast skin tightened. He obviously felt, from his point of view, that big boobs were great. In my twenties I was an introverted girl and wasn't up to criticising the 'god-like' doctor. My few wan complaints resulted in a referral to a psychiatrist! Obviously, to want smaller breasts was insane. Blonde hair and big boobs can make some women feel empowered but not me. I just felt embarrassed by my too-obvious curves. Introverts don't want to be stared at. They prefer to fly under the radar.

One of the few advantages of getting older is that you become invisible. This suited me just fine! But I still have problems with my oversized breasts. Over the years, the weight of them on my frame has resulted in a rare back problem, which means I can no longer wear a bra. My breasts are still too large to go without, so I now have to wear bodysuits. The largest cup size available in a size to fit the rest of my body is 12DD. As I am an F to G cup, I bulge out of the top. It's the same with swimsuits but by now I'm used to it.

I am amazed by the number of women going through surgery to get bigger boobs. From my point of view, they're very uncomfortable, both physically and psychologically.

Breast history

Ancient Greece and Rome: The ideal was smaller, more modest breasts that symbolised purity, youth and natural beauty.

Renaissance: A celebration of fuller, more voluptuous figures, representing fertility and abundance. The larger bust was a status symbol linked to robust health.

Victorian era: The hourglass figure emerged, aided by tight corsets, accentuating the bust without focusing on the natural size of the breasts.

1920s: The flapper era favoured a boyish, flat-chested appearance as women moved toward freedom and independence, rejecting the previous era's formality.

1950s: A return to curvy figures, with Marilyn Monroe epitomising the full bust and tiny waist. This era celebrated femininity and glamour.

1960s–1970s: The rise of the natural look, with the feminist movement rejecting rigid beauty standards. The braless movement popularised less emphasis on breast size and shape.

1980s–1990s: Surge in popularity of large, often surgically enhanced breasts, fuelled by fitness culture and celebrities like Pamela Anderson.

Modern era: The ideal has evolved to include both natural and enhanced breasts, with a growing trend toward body positivity that embraces diverse shapes and sizes. Celebrities like Kim Kardashian have influenced the rise of more sculpted, curvier figures.

Popular breast types

Round: Often achieved with implants; symmetrical and full, offering a prominent, enhanced look.

Teardrop: Fuller at the bottom and tapered at the top, resembling natural breasts.

Athletic: Smaller, firmer breasts often found in women who are fit or muscular.

Asymmetrical: A common natural variation where one breast is larger than the other, increasingly understood as part of normal body diversity.

CHAPTER THIRTY-ONE

Our contemporary fixation with symmetry

Breast implants have become increasingly popular for their ability to create symmetrical breasts. Symmetry, however, naturally varies among individuals. Human breasts are often asymmetrical; differences in size, shape and position are common and completely normal. However, modern beauty standards have usually emphasised symmetry, a concept that has deep psychological and cultural roots.

Ideals of beauty often equate symmetry with perfection and attractiveness. Studies in evolutionary biology suggest that humans are naturally drawn to symmetrical features. This preference is thought to stem from the way we tend to associate symmetry with health, genetic fitness and reproductive success. Symmetrical features might signal that a person has developed without significant genetic or environmental stressors, which may make them seem to be a healthier and more suitable mate.

In the realm of aesthetics, symmetry is often equated with beauty. This principle extends beyond human features to art, architecture and design. Symmetry provides a sense of balance and harmony that is pleasing to the eye. This aesthetic principle has been ingrained in various cultures throughout history. For instance, classical Greek art and architecture heavily emphasised symmetry, considering it a key element of beauty and proportion—think the Parthenon (structural) or the Venus de Milo (sculptural).

The media and celebrity culture also play a substantial role in promoting the ideal of symmetrical breasts. Celebrities often undergo breast augmentation to achieve a perfect, symmetrical bust, which is then showcased on screen, in magazines and on social media. These images create and reinforce beauty standards that influence how we perceive beauty and, as a result, many people seek cosmetic surgery. Breast implants are designed to achieve a more symmetrical appearance by addressing size discrepancies and providing a uniform shape. Surgeons can now select implants of different sizes and shapes for each breast to ensure a balanced appearance, correcting natural asymmetry.

The fixation on symmetrical breasts can also be linked to the psychology of self-image and confidence. Women with asymmetrical breasts can sometimes feel self-conscious or dissatisfied with their appearance. In these cases, breast implants may enhance confidence and body image. This psychological benefit is a significant motivating factor for many who choose to undergo breast augmentation. In addition, they might also struggle with finding the right bra, which are also made for symmetrical cup sizes!

Natural asymmetry of breasts is, believe it or not, perfectly normal and the pursuit of perfect symmetry is a societal construct rather than a necessity. Body-positivity movements emphasise embracing natural variations and rejecting unrealistic beauty standards. These movements encourage us to appreciate our bodies, including natural asymmetries, and challenge the notion that perfection means beauty.

But are we buying it? With cosmetic surgery on an exponential rise, are we any closer to accepting our asymmetrical bodies just as they are?

• • •

CHAPTER THIRTY-TWO

Actually, no one cares

Amanda

Enough about my boobs, for now. I'm sure you're probably a bit concerned that you know much more about my mammary glands than you'd really like to. What I think you all secretly want to know about is my time as an escort.

While I've recounted funny, sad and shocking stories in my books, I haven't really said too much about the escort agency I founded at the height of my fame (notoriety?) as Samantha X. OnlyFans stars and porn stars flood social media these days, but not too much is said about old-school escort agencies, the ones that employed older women who wouldn't even pose for a selfie, let alone have their bazookas and coochies splashed all over TikTok.

In my agency, Samantha X Angels, I employed mostly women over 40. Most of them were looking for a way out of their corporate jobs and wanting to change professions to something they believed was empowering and flexible, and – let's call a spade a spade here – something that would make them lots of money.

While preserving their identities, I can tell you the women who approached me for work were great (mostly). I had the odd one who stole clients, who turned up for work pissed, and even a Single White Female, but overall they were a jolly lot – warm, genuine and easygoing. Being older in this game was always a bonus. 'Mature and curvy' were the two most popular requests from eager men, who were willing to part with up to $800 for an hour with one of my 'Angels'.

Yes, you read correctly – 'mature and curvy'. Not 'young and skinny', or 'perfect body', or 'big fake boobs', or 'bouncy Brazilian backpacker with big bum' (although there is a market for everything, I can assure you). But older – good company, likes a yarn, doesn't look like their client's daughter on dinner dates – and *curvy*, which means a little cushion for the pushin'. And, as for the boobs, they didn't care.

Yup. *They didn't care*.

Small boobs, floppy boobs, inverted nipples, huge nipples, big and fake boobs, small and silicone boobs ... you name it. Men didn't care. I think most of them were just grateful to be in the company of a woman. There is a big difference between what men see as 'sexy' and what women *assume* men think is sexy. And it might surprise you, because it sure as hell surprised me!

I was one of those women who liked to impress men. I wanted to win the validation of men for lots of reasons – like low self-esteem. I dressed in tight clothes, showing off every dip, curve and flash of boobie, thinking that's what made me sexy, that's what men desired. Therefore, I thought, if men desired me, I was desirable and worthy of love.

So, when I first started in the adult industry, I assumed I had to be perfect. No wrinkles, no excess weight, no stretch marks, absolutely no cellulite, and of course *humungous* boobs. Then I heard it straight from the horse's mouth – from clients booking the Angels, from my own lovely clients, from men of all demographics (from teachers to bankers, tradies to cops): the type of women these men preferred were in fact very natural, they were certainly not perfect, and they definitely didn't have to have a certain-sized boob. 'Just someone I can talk to,' they always nervously asked for.

I've said it more than once – connection, not sex, was the number one reason men paid for sex workers. Quite remarkably, sex work isn't about sex. It's about connection between one human being and another, regardless of what size bra cup one of you (or both of you) wears.

The women I employed, and those who did well, were very natural-looking, surgery-free and Botox-free. Their bodies were by no means perfect, and they were quite often aged 45 and upwards. As we know, Mother Nature works her magic as we clock up the years, but our clients didn't care. In fact, I actually think they found it a turn-on. I'm not going to psychoanalyse them to find out why, but if I did, I'd bet my bottom dollar that floppy, natural boobs kind of reminded them of their mums, of breastfeeding, of feeling nurtured and loved and warm and safe and fuzzy inside ... you get my drift.

The women that did well in my agency were those who oozed confidence regardless of how they looked. More often than not, they were all natural. They had natural bodies, they were warm and they genuinely enjoyed the company of men.

These women, and the clients too, taught me a lesson no one had taught me before: you are enough the way you are. And secondly, no one honestly cares that much about the size of your boobs. They really don't. It took me five, maybe six boob jobs and lots of angst, faux validation, and a lot of time and energy spent worrying about the size of my chest to find out that, really, *no one cares*.

I don't know about you, but I find that rather refreshing.

• • •

CHAPTER THIRTY-THREE

'She's going to regret that!'

Ray was a queer colleague of mine with a passion for social justice. We worked together on all of the 'woke' projects that no one else wanted to work on. From Aboriginal and Torres Strait Islander traditional fishing, through to integrating LGBTQIA+ values into a right-wing corporate code of conduct: we were the people for the task. And we attacked it with the kind of vainglorious gusto that only the pious can muster.

One day we were visiting a strange but very well-known artist in his studio (more like a den) in Parramatta. We had tasked him with creating a sculpture for the opening of a luxury brand.

We had tasked said artist some six weeks before, and paid him a sizeable advance. Since then, he had produced absolutely nothing: a big fat zero. With the launch fast approaching, we were in desperate need of progress. Tangible progress we could demonstrate to the client.

Ray and I, besties in woke work, decided we might need to visually check in on said progress, particularly because the artist in question had a predilection for ice pipes ... or so we had heard on the Sydney grapevine.

But when he greeted us out the front in his signature colourful, loose clothes, kaftan style, he seemed perfectly, well, sober. His dark hair was perfectly styled, and he was clear of eye.

'Come in! I'll show you what I've been working on,' he declared, leading us through a garage – notably lacking in drug paraphernalia.

As we joined him in his equally small courtyard, we spotted the sculpture – strange but arresting.

We moved closer.

'This is my assistant, Barbara,' the artist announced, flinging an arm around her shoulder. Barbara seemed an odd name for such a young thing.

She smiled, and blew smoke in our faces. 'We're having the best time creating this thing!' She widened her arms to gesture to the structure.

I bet, I thought, but tried to suspend judgement.

But my eyes ... they floated down to her chest ... undignifiedly!

Similar to said famous artist, she was wearing a singlet. But under said singlet, she had two very large breasts that were clearly not strapped into any sort of bra. They jostled about excitedly.

Look away! my mind commanded.

I did, straight into her eyes instead.

'Wow! It looks fantastic!' I cried.

'Fantastic!' Ray responded, pushing his tortoiseshell sunglasses up his nose and casting a prim, surreptitious gaze towards the errant, freed breasts.

'Imagine it ...' the artist said, now gathering Ray and I both up under his arms '... spray-painted in hot pink.'

'Will there be glitter?' Ray asked, as we were both thrust too close for comfort to said 'thing'.

'Mass amounts of glitter,' the artist responded, now embracing Barbara.

Ray and I smiled tightly, uncomfortably, hoping our eyes wouldn't meet the bosoms.

'We love it,' we both cooed, woke and ridiculous.

Later, in the Uber heading back to the office: 'I like his vision for the whole thing,' I muttered.

'Yes ... indeed ... it's very camp, people will love it.'

'Agreed.'

'At least there were no pipes ... or evidence of pipes.'

'Absolutely.'

A long pause, as we shifted into Redfern.

'But ... she's going to regret that,' Ray said, in a jaunty tone.

'Him?' I inquired.

'No, darling ... he's her insurance policy. I mean, the no-bra thing.'

'What?' I gawped, shocked.

'The no-bra thing, babe. They are going to droop like nobody's business.'

I stared at him ... and almost said, 'Like your balls will?' But the words dissipated, lost in imagined retributions from HR.

'Really? I can't imagine,' I said instead.

'Darling,' he said, patting my hand, 'it's because you have small breasts. They never droop. But big, real boobs ... they do.'

• • •

CHAPTER THIRTY-FOUR

Droopy, real boobs

You might remember our homage to boob droopage at the start of this book.

The topic of braless breasts and how they droop, especially in contrast to fake breasts, is an intriguing one. Natural, larger breasts tend to droop more noticeably when unsupported, while surgically enhanced breasts often maintain a more lifted appearance, even without a bra. This difference arises from the fundamental structural variations between natural and augmented breasts.

Natural breasts are composed primarily of glandular tissue, fat and connective tissue, all of which are subject to the effects of gravity over time. The degree to which natural breasts droop, or sag, depends on several factors, including genetics, age, pregnancy, breastfeeding, weight fluctuations and overall skin elasticity. Larger breasts have more mass, making them more susceptible to gravitational pull, leading to a more pronounced droop when unsupported. This natural sagging is a normal part of aging and varies significantly from person to person.

When women go braless, the ligaments and skin in their breasts take on the full weight, leading to more noticeable sagging in larger, natural breasts. Bras provide support by redistributing the weight of the breasts, reducing the strain on the Cooper's ligaments and skin, which helps maintain a perkier appearance. Without this support, the natural elasticity of the skin and ligaments is tested, leading to more visible drooping, particularly in larger breasts.

In contrast, breast implants behave differently. Implants are placed either above or below the chest muscle. The structure and placement help maintain a firm, lifted shape, even without a bra. The material of the implants does not sag in the same way as natural breast tissue, and the surrounding scar tissue (called 'capsular contracture') can provide additional support. Consequently, fake breasts tend to retain their shape and position better without a bra when compared to natural breasts.

Cultural perceptions and preferences play a significant role in how we view breast sagging. Society often idolises youthful, perky breasts, which leads many women to have their breasts augmented, or to wear supportive bras and undergarments. These are perceived to offer a more aesthetically pleasing appearance without the need for constant support. It's essential, though, to acknowledge the practical aspects of living with larger, natural breasts. Many women with larger busts experience discomfort or pain when going braless due to the lack of support. This can lead to back, shoulder and neck pain, making bras not just a tool for aesthetic enhancement but also a necessity for physical comfort and health. On the other hand, women with fake breasts often do not face the same level of discomfort when going braless, as the implants provide inherent support.

The body-positivity movement challenges these traditional norms, encouraging us to accept natural breast shapes and sizes, including the natural drooping that comes with larger breasts. This shift promotes the idea that all bodies are beautiful, regardless of whether they fit the conventional standards of perkiness and symmetry.

• • •

CHAPTER THIRTY-FIVE

Breastfeeding, judging and sagging

'I think I'll just go with this one,' I said to my friend Sacha. It was a pastel-blue evening gown, with a corset and a high split. I didn't usually wear this colour, but it suited my tanned complexion remarkably well.

'You look good in anything,' Sacha told me, as the assistant pushed and tucked her into a beige, strapless beaded gown. It was utterly stunning, but one size too small, and they didn't have the size up in the store.

'Thanks,' I responded. This was standard women's dialogue: put a tall, skinny, flat-chested woman in anything and the women will coo in approval.

'Clothes horse,' someone would eventually utter.

Put that same woman – me, in this case – in a room full of men, and only the queer ones would notice her.

'I love this beaded number on you,' I responded, taking a seat on the pouf directly behind us, while she turned to view herself at a number of angles.

We were going to another friend's wedding, and the dress code was black tie.

'You think? I'm just not sure what it will look like in the bigger size,' she said, undoing her hair from its hair tie and letting it cascade around her, as if this might change the appearance of the dress.

Women: we only ever try on a swimsuit with heels, and a formal dress with our hair out. It's an optical illusion of sorts, the analogue version of a filter.

The predicament here? What the dress would look like in a larger size. The sales assistant had informed us that to order in the larger size, a down payment would have to be made. On a dress that cost well into the thousands of dollars, this was a considerable commitment.

'I'm sure it will look fabulous,' I encouraged from my seated position. Everyone needs a little encouragement in the change room. I channelled my best sales-assistant energy, garnered from my days working at Miranda Westfield in my teen years.

'I'm worried about my boobs,' Sacha suddenly declared.

'Why?' This was the last thing I'd expected. I knew Sacha well and she usually directed her negative-body-image thinking towards her stomach or thighs. Back in the day, when we had been inseparable at university, she had always been the boob girl and I had been the leg girl. The perfect combination hookup- or friend-wise – diverse strengths, and unlikely to attract the same man.

'Well, the tummy ... I can just get one of those tummy-training corset things that just sucks everything in. But the boobs ... ever since I breastfed Ava, they are droopy, they're like two old sacks, and even if I wear something that hoists them up, they still lack a certain buoyancy.'

'I doubt it ...' I muttered, having never really considered Sacha's boobs in such depth.

‘Babe, you don’t get it ... you have small boobs, and you didn’t really breastfeed.’

‘I breastfed for a little while,’ I say, a little indignantly.

‘You breastfed for a couple of months, if that – I breastfed for years. You don’t get it.’

I tried not to take it personally.

‘I’m sure you can find a bra that will work with that dress,’ I said instead, really having no idea in this space but trying to say the right thing.

‘I can’t take that risk. I might end up with these two flaccid sacks just jammed into this expensive dress.’ She looked distraught.

‘Don’t say that,’ I said, hating the negative energy that had just infiltrated our fun Girls’ Day space.

She whipped around and said, ‘It’s true. You know that if I leave Paul, or if he leaves me, I’m going to have my boobs done and my tummy tucked?’

This had taken a turn ...

‘Doctor Moradi said they’re his most popular surgeries,’ I found myself saying by way of response.

‘I’m not surprised,’ she said throwing her hands up in exasperation. ‘This is what happens after you have kids.’

I opened and closed my mouth, fish-like, trying to find something to say. Open, close. Open, close. Open, close.

She took this as a sign that I had verified her point.

‘Listen,’ she said snippily to the twenty-something sales assistant with pert boobs and luminescent skin. ‘I need something in a size twelve. I can’t just order something and not know what it looks like. Okay?’

The sales assistant looked mildly terrified, but she

recovered herself. 'Yes, absolutely, I'll find something.'

'And not in bottle green,' Sacha commanded. 'My high-school uniform was bottle green. I can't wear anything in that colour.'

The sales assistant's face turned from left to right, left to right, desperately looking for something that might meet the criteria.

I jumped in, hoping to help, and gestured towards the dress I was wearing: 'I'll take this one!' She didn't register what I was saying and raced off looking for a size 12 in a non-bottle green shade.

'Right, well, I'll get changed then,' I said, heading into the change room.

In the privacy of the change room, my mind stumbled on Sacha's comment: 'If I leave Paul, or if he leaves me, I'm going to have my boobs done ...' Strangely, it married up with my partner's comments: 'As long as you're not getting them done to meet someone else.'

Were augmented breasts required to meet the future love of your life? Were existing partners expected to simply put up with our errant, natural breasts, whether drooping or non-existent?

And why did new partners require augmented breasts?

Take note here: augmented breasts don't actually look like real breasts. Real breasts are uneven; they can be small or medium, and random in shape, texture and volume. Augmented breasts ... are quite clearly augmented breasts. So, in the age of porn, do we need augmented breasts to meet a man?

• • •

CHAPTER THIRTY-SIX

Women (and men) judge you if you don't breastfeed

'Lisa.' This was followed by a long-exasperated sigh. 'I need your help. I have a really fucking unhappy client.'

It was 8 a.m. and Leah, a junior social media advisor, had called me from her mobile. I was already in the office by then, having dropped off a daughter to before-school care and a one-year-old son to the mother-in-law.

'What happened?'

'Okay ... so it's the health organisation.'

Our government client. The kind of client that paid big and didn't expect much. The kind of client we liked to keep happy.

'What happened?'

'Well, it's bloody World Breastfeeding Week ... and I posted a celebratory post for them on socials about breastfeeding, and then I added a couple of milk emojis. One was the bottle of milk emoji.'

I knew the one.

'Anyway, they called me this morning, at seven a.m., saying they can absolutely not be seen to be promoting bottle feeding.'

'What?'

'Yes, apparently the World Health Organization says you're supposed to breastfeed until a baby is two.'

'Really? Seems rather odd ... they have actual teeth then.'

'Do they?'

'Yes, like a full-on set of teeth,' I reinforced, slightly horrified.

'Well ... true story. And they are very angry. They want me to pull the whole post down. It's had five thousand likes ... and some ten thousand views!'

'Okay ... this is crazy. What about women who can't breastfeed? Like there are women out there who literally can't!'

'I know ... they said take it down.'

'Hang on ... there's no fucking boob-and-baby-sucking emoji. Can't we argue that this is the only emoji that is fit for purpose?' I continued, incensed by the radical nature of this demand, and perhaps taking it a little personally.

'I tried that too.'

'Nothing?'

'They said if we don't take it down they're contacting the managing director!'

I rolled my eyes.

'Fuck,' I conceded.

'Take it down?' she inquired.

'Take it down,' I confirmed.

• • •

CHAPTER THIRTY-SEVEN

The World Health Organization and breastfeeding

The World Health Organization (WHO) has long advocated for breastfeeding as the optimal method of feeding infants, for both the health of the child and of the breastfeeding mother. According to WHO guidelines, infants should be exclusively breastfed for the first six months of life, followed by continued breastfeeding along with appropriate complementary foods for up to two years or beyond. This advice is rooted in substantial evidence demonstrating the myriad benefits of breastfeeding, including improved nutrition for the baby, enhanced immune protection and stronger mother–child bonding. However, while these recommendations are well intentioned and supported by scientific research, they can also be perceived as prescriptive, potentially disregarding the diverse circumstances and challenges faced by many women and families.

Controversial opinion: how much of this is also rooted in the control of women's bodies?

Breastfeeding is widely recognised for its health benefits. It provides essential nutrients, antibodies and hormones that help protect infants against common childhood illnesses and chronic conditions. The act of breastfeeding fosters a unique emotional bond between mother and child, contributing to the psychological and emotional development of infants. For mothers, breastfeeding is associated with a reduced risk of breast and ovarian cancers, type 2 diabetes and post-natal depression. Economically, breastfeeding reduces healthcare costs and the need for formula milk, which can be a significant expense for families.

Despite these advantages, the WHO's breastfeeding guidelines can inadvertently impose a form of 'policing' on women's bodies. The term 'policing' here refers to pressures and expectations that dictate how women should use their bodies, often disregarding individual circumstances and autonomy. By promoting breastfeeding for two years as the ideal, these guidelines can create a sense of obligation and guilt among mothers who, for various reasons, may not be able to adhere to this standard. Women who struggle with breastfeeding due to medical conditions, lack of support or personal choice might feel judged or inadequate. This can exacerbate feelings of stress and anxiety, overshadowing the importance of a mother's mental health and wellbeing.

Not all women can breastfeed. Medical conditions such as insufficient glandular tissue, previous breast surgeries or certain chronic illnesses can make breastfeeding difficult or impossible. Additionally, some mothers may face psychological barriers, such as a history of trauma or severe postnatal depression, that make breastfeeding a challenging or undesirable option. Socioeconomic factors also play a role; women in low-income settings or those who must return to work shortly after giving birth may find it impractical to breastfeed for extended periods.

In this context, the WHO's guidelines may inadvertently contribute to stigmatisation and discrimination against women who use formula feeding. The narrative that 'breast is best' can overshadow the validity of formula as a safe and nutritious alternative. Formula feeding can be a necessary and practical choice for many families, and it is important to acknowledge that the ultimate goal should be the health and wellbeing of both mother and child, rather than adherence to a singular feeding method.

Would it be possible to actually look after our children (and our bodies!) as we see fit?

The guidelines also fail to adequately consider the experiences of same-sex male couples who are raising infants. In these families, breastfeeding is not an option, and the reliance on formula or donor milk becomes essential. The exclusive focus on breastfeeding in public health messaging can marginalise these families, making them feel excluded from the broader discourse on infant nutrition. It is crucial for health organisations to provide inclusive and supportive guidance that recognises and respects diverse family structures and feeding practices.

Furthermore, the practical challenges of breastfeeding are often underestimated. Effective breastfeeding requires adequate support, education and resources. In many parts of the world, especially in low- and middle-income countries, women lack access to lactation consultants, breastfeeding-friendly workplaces and social support networks. This gap between policy and practice can leave women feeling unsupported and overwhelmed. Policies that advocate for extended breastfeeding must be accompanied by robust support systems, including paid maternity leave, breastfeeding-friendly public spaces and accessible healthcare services.

It is also important to consider the cultural dimensions of breastfeeding. In some cultures, breastfeeding in public is stigmatised, and women may face social pressure to stop breastfeeding earlier than recommended. Conversely, in other cultures, breastfeeding is a norm and formula feeding is frowned upon. Public health recommendations should be sensitive to these cultural contexts and strive to promote infant nutrition in a way that is respectful and inclusive of different cultural practices and beliefs.

A balanced and inclusive framework should prioritise all families making informed choices, and being supported regardless of their feeding method. Health organisations should provide accurate information about the benefits of breastfeeding while also validating and supporting alternative feeding choices. This includes promoting the availability of donor milk, improving access to high-quality formula, and ensuring that all parents receive the guidance and support they need to make the best decisions for their families. By fostering an environment of support and understanding, we can better promote the health and wellbeing of all children and families.

• • •

CHAPTER THIRTY-EIGHT

You know you're breastfeeding when ...

- You meticulously plan your workday, holidays and even date nights around your pumping schedule like it's a life-or-death mission.
- Knit shirts? Stretched to oblivion from your toddler's self-service grabs.
- Your wardrobe is now dominated by shirts that open in the front – fashionably functional, or just plain necessary?
- Every single shirt you own has at least one telltale stain from surprise leaks. It's the new normal.
- Sitting next to you sometimes comes with a splash zone warning.
- That awkward moment when you realise you've been walking around the house with one boob still hanging out.

- Spilling even a single drop of milk feels like a tragedy of Shakespearean proportions.
- You've mastered the fine art of repurposing breastmilk to cure everything from sunburns to ear infections. Miracle elixir, anyone?
- Your partner wakes up to an unexpected 'peep show' but you're passed out, blissfully unaware.
- Hearing a baby cry in public triggers a panicked thought: 'Did I put on my breast pads today?'
- You're grateful for limo tint on your car windows because your car doubles as your mobile pumping sanctuary.
- You pack your breast pump for a 10-kilometre run or a Vegas trip without hesitation. Times have truly changed.
- Hunger, exhaustion, toddler drama? Whip out the boob – it's the ultimate problem solver.
- Heading out the front door includes a reflexive chest check to ensure everything's covered.

• • •

CHAPTER THIRTY-NINE

So long, Samantha X

Amanda

With great power comes great responsibility. Okay, that's a quote from *Spider-Man*, but if you replace the word 'power' with 'breasts', and replace the word 'responsibility' with 'power', you will come to understand that having great big tits gives you great big power over men.

That's right. *Power*. Women may snigger and judge, but men? They may say loudly how fake I look, how terrible, how off-putting, but I can assure you, ladies, men *love* tits. The bigger, the better – fake or natural. And do not believe a single straight man who says they don't, because of course they're going to say that to you, their smaller-breasted partner who they genuinely love very much, because you are wife material and I am not. Believe me: they wank to big tits. They don't necessarily want the woman they love to have big fakies, but in their fantasies, they're thinking about them.

And I had the evidence. I had the biggest boobs I could possibly have (any bigger and they'd have to be imported from America – no joke). I was a walking social experiment. Men became obsessed with my breasts. Men stared. Men followed me home (yes, that happened). My DMs were mostly about my breasts ('The best in Australia!'). It was quite the accolade. Me! The ugly friend who had to grow some tits now had 'the best in Australia'! Fancy that.

A few of my clients commented that they were too big – just not 'classy'. These were clients I'd known for years and had become good friends with. But on dates, in my real life? Men's eyes lit up like Christmas trees. It was almost comical. *Wow. Men really are like little kids*, I remember thinking, watching a young surfer's eyes brighten as he gazed at my chest while we chatted at the beach. *So simple. So visual. So easy.*

When I accidentally drove through a red light, I was let off by a cop after I quickly undid a button on my top. I got out of parking tickets by heaving my chest and apologising profusely. Doors opened (literally), men smiled, men stared, men nudged their mates. One man ran up to me in the street and asked for my number. (I was wearing a boob tube and baggy trousers. It wasn't the trousers, I can assure you.) I felt like the Pied Piper of Men. Tradies who did work on my house didn't even hide their lingering glances.

I had a piece of fitness equipment delivered to my

house and the installer's eyes popped out of his head when he glanced at my boobs. 'I'd love to have sex with you on this equipment,' he murmured.

I shot him a look. *Did he really say that?* I wasn't sure. But he was staring at my boobs. My face flushed and I was too shocked to make some smart-arse comment. But this felt like my fault. I had created this big-boobed monster, and I knew (most) men were pretty basic.

And of course it was a buzz! Being insecure and needing validation from men, I *loved* the surge of electricity, ego and power. *Aged late forties and still got it!*

When I was feeling down and I wanted an ego hit, I'd put on a tight T-shirt and go for a walk. The attention was addictive. I felt powerful. I felt sexy. I felt womanly. The feeling was like a hit of cocaine fizzing through my body.

The thing with any drug, though, is the downer. What goes up has to come down.

A male friend – platonic – came over one lunchtime and, for the sake of cutting a long story short (plus it's in *Misfit* in all its glory), he confessed he had an addiction to 'big fake tits' and admitted he would 'last three seconds if I took my top off'. This was a man I had loved chewing the fat with about politics, media and advertising. He has since apologised but it was the final straw. Men were never, ever going to take me seriously, were they?

Another man wanted to see me naked to 'see how he felt about his girlfriend'.

I heard a barista refer to me as 'the blonde with the big tits'. I mean, no lie there, but that wasn't all I had to offer the world. Not to mention the looks and judgement from other women.

The validation from men was something that actually fast became a little boring, shallow and annoying. I would forever be the woman men wanted to fuck but not date – and I put it all down to the size of my breasts. My job and reputation as a high-profile escort didn't help my dating life either, but that's another story and another book.

It was during this era – the 1050cc breasts era, which lasted a couple of years – that I decided to retire from escorting. I would put Samantha X to bed (so to speak) and become Amanda Goff again. I had been diagnosed with bipolar II, was on the right medication and life had settled down for me. I was no longer searching for fame and fortune. I was getting tired of having to be 'sexy', and I wanted a relationship and a normal life – as normal as I could possibly cope with, anyway.

The news of my retirement made headlines, and the usual lingerie photos from years ago resurfaced (cringe). But I knew that, like all other salacious news stories, mine would soon be tomorrow's fish-and-chips wrapper. A few days of sensationalist headlines, the usual cutting *Daily Mail* comments and that was it. I had decided to follow my dream of becoming a Pilates teacher, and I hung up the high heels with a sense of relief.

I could begin my life as Amanda Goff. And it felt fantastic.

There was just one problem. Or, shall we say, two problems. Guess what they were ...

The thing is, when I put Samantha to bed, she no longer existed. I shed her skin – but not all of it. While I was Amanda, every time I looked in the mirror, or tried to dress myself nicely, my huge breasts were a constant reminder.

I felt my clothes looked stupid on me – too tight, and they no longer looked right.

I felt cheap. The attention from men was still there but I no longer appreciated the stares. I had launched my podcast *Xposed* and was back to being a journalist again. I filmed the episodes and cringed as my boobs were there, staring right back at me and dominating the frame.

My body no longer fitted the image. My boobs felt like they didn't belong anymore. It was no longer me, or the person I was trying to become.

Studying Pilates and wearing activewear, going to the studio and working out, I felt even more out of place. I covered up in baggy T-shirts and felt extremely self-conscious. Then on the days I got a bit of attention – a wink, a smile, a flirt – and I felt good, I made it all about my boobs.

I loved them or I hated them, depending on my mood. I asked men, I asked women, I asked gay friends: *Should I get rid of the boobs?* I didn't get a definite answer. *Yes. No. Maybe. Just leave them. They're part of you now.* Blah blah.

It was a never-ending fucking cycle and it was draining.

I chatted to a highly influential woman I knew who made a comment about my breasts too. 'I presume you will get those breasts reduced now?' she said with a smile, referring to my recent retirement.

'Yes, yes I will,' I replied, smiling sweetly but burning inside. *Here we go again.* If I wanted women to like me, I'd have to get them reduced. If I wanted men to desire me, I'd have to keep them. I had made my boobs mean something. *I* had made my boobs define me.

• • •

CHAPTER FORTY

Antigone

In Greek mythology, Antigone is a tragic but courageous heroine. Born to Oedipus, the tragic king of Thebes, and his mother-wife Jocasta, the young Antigone rebels against the laws of man in favour of the laws of her gods. As Sophocles tells it in his iconic tragedy *Antigone*, she defies King Creon, her uncle, who forbids the burial of her brother Polynices. For Antigone, the sacred rites of family and respect for the goddesses and gods transcend the will of any king, no matter how powerful. Her determination to do what she believes is right leads to her eventual death, but it also cements her legacy as a symbol of bravery, strength and moral conviction.

Fast-forward to modern times and we find a woman who seems to share many of these same qualities. Antigone, affectionately known as Tig, is a force of nature. She's been introduced to me through my good friend Belinda, who knows that I'm deeply interested in speaking with women who have experienced mastectomies. 'Tig,' Belinda tells me, 'is like a powerful angel – a woman who combines kindness with a fiery spirit. She's both empathetic and a force to be reckoned with.' Intrigued, I set up a meeting with Tig. However, as is often the case with small children and unforeseen illnesses, the meeting turns into a phone call. Still, even through the mobile line, Tig's presence is palpable. You can feel her energy, the wisdom in her voice and the sheer life force that carries her through.

In many ways, Tig is like a living, breathing Antigone, her story unfolding with the kind of raw emotional depth that makes you realise that life itself is a series of tragic and triumphant moments, each shaping and reshaping who we are. It's the kind of narrative that quivers off the page, one you can't help but feel in your bones.

Tig begins by describing her breasts with the same reverence and contradiction one might attribute to an ancient artifact. 'My boobs were the most important part of me,' she tells me. 'They defined me, almost. They were GGs, which is pretty extraordinary and, as you can imagine, I loved them and hated them. I had three kids and they all loved to rest their heads down on them, and off they went to sleep. Big Greek mamma-type boobs! They meant warmth ... and, obviously, they were sexy. My partners loved them, and I knew they had a certain power over men. One look at the cleavage and they were entranced. They were something incredibly special, and a central part of me, for many years. Forty-two years, to be exact.'

Tig's story starts as she is driving up the coast of Queensland, on a summer road trip to visit her sister in Mission Beach. She's no stranger to the tropics – the warm waters, the sea lice, the occasional tropical ulcer. So when she notices sores around her nipples, she doesn't think much of it. 'I thought they were tropical ulcers,' she recalls. 'I'd just had a mammogram the previous November, and it was clear, but when I got back to Sydney in February 2002 and the ulcers hadn't healed, I thought it was a bit weird and should get it checked out.'

Turns out, it was more than just a tropical nuisance. Tig was diagnosed with ductal carcinoma in situ (DCIS), a form of breast cancer where the cancer cells are confined to the milk ducts. She had no idea if there was a family history of breast cancer – her father had passed away when she was still very young and, as with many first-generation migrants, he was estranged from his family in Greece. The knowledge wasn't there, and neither was the warning.

By May 2002, Tig made the decision to remove both breasts. Even though the cancer was contained in one breast, she opted for a bilateral mastectomy. The decision was radical, but ultimately the right one. 'It was radical,' she admits, 'but by the time I had the surgery, they had discovered cancer in both breasts.'

In the early 2000s, immediate breast reconstruction wasn't an option. It was recommended to wait five years, in case of secondary breast cancer. So, Tig went from GG breasts to absolutely nothing. It was a transformation of epic proportions, both physically and emotionally. But, surprisingly, Tig found freedom in this. 'To be honest, it was liberating,' she says, with a sense of calm I didn't expect. 'It was liberating to have no breasts, after a lifetime of being laboured by them, or having to have custom-made bras and all the rest. There was a certain freedom in it. I came out quite positive. When you've got kids, you can't wallow.'

It's easy to assume that the physical transformation would have been the hardest part. But for Tig, it was the pain and recovery afterward that took the biggest toll. 'The postoperative pain and rehabilitation were shocking,' she admits. 'The scar tissue, the oozing. I couldn't lift my arms to midway for a year, and I couldn't lift them all the way up for two years. I wasn't prepared for that. I had three kids, a partner, a job – it was debilitating. My body went straight into menopause, and everything changed. I developed lymphoedema' – a build-up of fluid in the body's tissues – 'and the pain was so bad on one side, in my arm and hand, that I got to a point where I asked the doctor whether getting my arm amputated would be a solution.'

It's here, in the midst of her pain, that Tig has a thought that jolts her into an almost surreal frame of mind. 'And that's when I first thought, *I'm going to die*,' she reflects. 'And that's when things got really strange.'

In her mind, death was no longer an abstract concept. She believed she was nearing the end, so she decided to make preparations for her family. 'I decided to move to Alice Springs – alone. I applied for two jobs, one in Cairns and one in Alice Springs, as a social worker. That was my background. Looking back, I was probably in a postoperative delusional state, but I thought I was going to die, and I wanted to prepare my family for living without me. I had the sense they couldn't do it alone.'

Despite her fears, Tig was offered both jobs, and she ended up in Alice Springs, where she lived in the nurses' quarters. 'Back then, we didn't have mobile phones, just a pager,' she laughs. 'The kids would message me, *Come back! Dad is starving us to death!* Jokes, of course, but it had an impact on them. My daughter, who was thirteen, would come from Sydney and visit me. She'd stay in the nurses' quarters. The nurses would tell her stories, give her nips of tequila. It was a different time, but there was a sense of sisterhood, and I think those experiences had a big impact on her.'

Tig's medical journey took an unusual turn. She didn't undergo radiation or chemotherapy, despite the oncologist's insistence. 'The oncologist was fixated on me getting it, but they had removed everything. I had undergone the most radical surgery. What more could be done?' she reasoned. 'I told her, "No, I'm not doing it."'

Her scars were still fresh, still painful, but Tig forged ahead. 'I had my breasts removed in May 2002, and by February 2003, I was working in Alice Springs. It was a crazy move, but I needed to do it. It was the right thing to do.'

After five months in Alice Springs, Tig returned to Sydney, where she rejoined her partner and children. 'By the time I went back to Sydney, my kids had at least some experience of life without Ma,' she says.

For her partner, it was a difficult transition as well. 'He was supportive of everything I went through, but it was a big loss for him too. Building up our intimacy again, after losing my breasts physically and spiritually, was huge. But we got there over time.'

Five years later, Tig underwent reconstruction surgery. She couldn't wait to have breasts again. 'If I could have done it sooner, I would have,' she admits. 'I went to this lovely Greek surgeon. I loved the team there. I could speak my native language, and they were so empathetic. He said to me, "Antigone, it's going to hurt. We're opening up old scars." But I wanted it done, so I went through with it. I had lovely Bs. But in hindsight, I wish I hadn't done it.'

The years since have been a whirlwind of medical challenges. In 2016 during a stormy night, a tree fell on Tig's car while she was in it, causing several injuries and a slow leak in one of her breast implants. This resulted in surgery for one breast implant replacement. In 2019, the other implant was found to be leaking, and she decided to have them both removed. Fortunately, Tig had access to a medicinal cannabis trial, which helped alleviate the pain and avoid the mental health struggles that other opiate-based painkillers had caused her.

Sadly, Tig's younger sister passed away last year after a battle with breast cancer, but despite all the trials, Tig remains a woman of strength, resilience and compassion. Her journey, much like in the classical tragedy *Antigone*, is one of defiance and the search for personal truth. She embodies strength in an inspiring and humbling way.

Now, in her mid-sixties, Tig reflects on her life. 'I look back and think, *My boobs were the most significant element of my life.* It seems ridiculous, but they were such a central part of my story. And they still are.'

• • •

CHAPTER FORTY-ONE

'That's so uncomfortable, right?'

The night was a swirl of neon hues and sparkling lights, a true Sydney Mardi Gras spectacle unfolding around me. The air was thick with excitement, buzzing with the hum of thousands of people. It was a puff of fairy floss and glitter, a celebration of everything from pure joy to unapologetic self-expression. I could feel the vibrations of the music pulsing through the crowd, each beat of the drum a call to the heart. It was impossible not to get swept up in it.

My friend and I had been planning this night for what felt like years, and here we were, the night still young, and everything around us already chaotic in the best way. We found ourselves inside the Colombian, a quintessential spot for anyone wanting to catch their breath amid the madness of Mardi Gras. A gin and tonic in my hand, my sequinned bra was catching the light with every movement. The short shorts I was wearing – because why not? – out-glittered all competition. But I wasn't alone in my full-on party ensemble. My friend, ever the partner in crime, had gone all out too. Her outfit was just as wild, just as unapologetic. She was wearing a brightly coloured fringed vest that swished around her body as she moved, paired with holographic pants that caught the light like a disco ball. If there was ever a moment to let go of inhibitions, this was it.

It wasn't just us, though. Around us, the diversity of the crowd was stunning. Some were wearing the quintessential Mardi Gras costume – a mix of feathers, sequins and glitter – while others were dressed in outfits that screamed rebellion, or maybe liberation. One person caught my attention: a figure standing just a bit too close to the bar. They were dressed in a sleek black bondage outfit, the straps crisscrossing their torso in an intricate, almost architectural fashion. It wasn't the outfit that caught my eye at first, though. It was the scars.

Clear, jagged lines marked their chest, the telltale signs of breast-removal surgery. I didn't stare – I couldn't, it felt too invasive – but it made me think. In the midst of all the glitter and the celebration of gender fluidity and expression, here was a body that spoke its own truth, its own battle, its own journey.

My friend leaned in, breaking my trance. Her voice was just above a whisper, but the concern in her tone was unmistakable. 'That's so uncomfortable, right?' she asked, nodding towards the person with the scars.

I tilted my head, watching for a moment as the individual turned, their face expressionless but resolute. 'What do you mean?' I asked, genuinely curious.

She shrugged, a flicker of uncertainty crossing her face. 'The whole ... thing. The outfit, the scars. It looks like it must be so uncomfortable. I don't think I could ever ... do that.'

I didn't respond immediately, unsure of where to go with it. Was she referring to the outfit itself, or was it something deeper? I took another sip of my gin and tonic. The drink burned a little less this time, as if my body had finally realised the magnitude of what was being said in this exchange.

'It's not about comfort,' I said slowly. 'It's about how we interact with our bodies.' I paused, trying to make sense of my thoughts. 'Breasts ... they're not just parts of us. They're tied to so much more – our identity, sexuality, gender, motherhood, even pain. It's like a whole story in one part of the body.'

She raised her eyebrows, intrigued, as she shifted her weight on the bar stool. 'Yeah, but still. Those scars ... aren't they uncomfortable?' She was looking at me now, almost searching for an answer to a question neither of us had fully articulated.

'Why uncomfortable?' I asked, slightly challenging her. 'Because they're a reminder of something painful? Of what? What do you think breasts are supposed to be? Are they supposed to be beautiful? Soft? Perfect? Aren't they all just pieces of flesh we don't get to decide how we feel about until something happens? A surgery, a choice, a moment of trauma or empowerment?'

She blinked, processing the words, and I could see her thinking, rethinking, the gears shifting behind her eyes. 'I guess,' she started, 'it's just that breasts are so ... linked to who we are as women, aren't they? Like, they're so tied to our identity.'

She didn't need to finish the thought. I knew exactly what she meant. Breasts are seen as symbols of fertility, of womanhood, of sex – and yet, in the same breath, they can be reduced to something commercial, an object to be bought, sold and shown off. We're taught to associate them with femininity, but at what cost? What happens when we take that symbol away, turn it into a scar, or strip it of its glossy, polished exterior?

The whole conversation felt heavier, but also, in a strange way, more comforting. My friend's words had struck a chord. She was right: breasts were these vessels that carried so many layers. To some, they were nurturing, soft, the source of life itself, while to others, they were instruments of pleasure, symbols of sex or simply another part of the body. They were subject to the gaze of others – whether that gaze was loving, lecherous or just plain neutral. And then there were those whose breasts didn't fit the narrative. Whose breasts had become something they no longer recognised, or perhaps never had. What did that mean for their identities?

And yet, we were standing in this celebration of liberation, of freedom, of the right to be whoever the hell we wanted to be. Mardi Gras, in all its glittering glory, was about throwing off the shame, about stripping away the social constructs and reclaiming the body – our bodies – on our own terms. My tonic fizzed in the glass as I took another sip.

'Look,' I said, nodding in the direction of the person with the scars again, my voice a little quieter now. 'I think the thing is, they're not uncomfortable with their body. They've made a decision. They've said, "I'm going to show up as I am, scars and all." And in a way, it's the opposite of uncomfortable. It's about embracing what's left, what's real.'

My friend's gaze softened, and for a moment she just stared at the person in the black bondage outfit, perhaps seeing them in a different light. It wasn't about what they wore or how they looked. It was about what they were saying.

'You're right,' she said after a beat. 'It's not uncomfortable, is it? It's just ... part of the story.'

I nodded. 'Exactly. Breasts, scars and everything in between. It's all part of the story.'

The music was louder now, the thump of bass reverberating through the floor beneath our feet. My friend grinned, the sparkle in her eyes matching the glitter of the crowd around us. 'You know,' she said, tapping her glass against mine in a celebratory clink, 'you're right. All the complicated parts of us – we can celebrate them, every single one.'

I couldn't help but smile. Mardi Gras, with its sequins, its confetti and its unapologetic joy, was the perfect backdrop for a conversation like this. Here, in the middle of all the madness, the only thing that truly mattered was the freedom to be who we were, and the freedom for everyone there to define themselves on our own terms. The rest – well, it was just fairy floss and glitter.

• • •

CHAPTER FORTY-TWO

Explaining to people that you're writing a book on boobs

Explaining that I'm writing a book on boobs has become a conversation starter of its own, often leading to a bizarre but endlessly entertaining range of reactions. Men, in particular, seem to get very ... pink. It's as though the conversation is a sudden bright light in a room they were unaware was even dimly lit. You can almost hear the gears grinding as they search for the appropriate response, which is usually some variation of humour.

'Well, that's a book that will write itself!' one might laugh, eyes darting anywhere but my face. Or, 'That's a book I'll be buying!' – and while I do appreciate the enthusiasm, it's always delivered in a tone that suggests I might be part of some underground publishing phenomenon. Even better, there's the odd 'Will there be pictures?' It's like a joke they're trying to make, but everyone is secretly hoping the answer is yes.

Women, on the other hand, are intrigued, and rightly so. There's always a palpable sense of curiosity in their voices as they lean in. Every time I share my book project, it's as though I've just handed them a golden key to a secret door. They can't wait to share their own stories, their own thoughts or even the sheer realisation of how little we talk about boobs – how little space these parts of our bodies really take up in our larger social discourse, despite how much we think about them. And when I tell people about the book, the conversation often spirals into unexpected directions, like some strange, titillating game of telephone. It's no longer just about boobs; it's about how they're seen, experienced, objectified and everything in between.

One evening, a friend and her partner came over for dinner. The night was shaping up to be fairly standard until I decided to break the seal and mention the book. It was casual, as casual as something as potentially uncomfortable as discussing boobs can be. We were sitting on my rental sofa – a story in itself, because my recliner sofa had exploded the week before, adding a particularly chaotic touch to my life that I wasn't entirely prepared for – when the boob-book topic came up. And the reaction? Well, as I anticipated, it was a mixed bag.

My friend's partner quickly and conspicuously looked down, probably unsure of how to process this sudden eruption of ... breast talk. Meanwhile, my friend – bless her enthusiasm – was visibly excited, leaning forward, her face glowing with a curious kind of delight. She was cradling her glass of chardonnay like she had just been handed the most fascinating piece of gossip.

'Wow! That is so exciting!' she exclaimed.

I, however, felt the heat rise in my own cheeks, and not just because of the wine. There's something about talking about breasts – our breasts, someone else's breasts – that makes people squirm. So, I launched into my explanation of what the book would be: a sociocultural exploration of boobs. From history to the contemporary obsession with the pornification of the female body, with a strong undercurrent of personal stories from women about their own breasts. It was as though a wave of seriousness rolled over me as I spoke, yet at the same time, I couldn't shake the sense that this was a subject no one was quite prepared for.

Her partner excused himself, retreating quietly outside where my partner was working the barbecue. I couldn't help but wonder if, for him, the world of boobs was just a little too much to handle. Maybe it was safer to stick to the more familiar terrain of grilling meats, which, I suppose, doesn't come with the same complicated, multilayered discourse as the female breast. I continued, undeterred.

'This is so great,' my friend said, again leaning forward as though I had just handed her a profound new way of seeing the world.

'I never really thought about boobs until I met Amanda, really, and then it became obvious that they were so powerful,' I admitted.

Her eyebrow arched in confusion. 'Hang on – you never thought about your boobs?'

This wasn't the first time I'd been asked this question. Women who have large breasts often have a very different relationship with their bodies than I do. Their experiences are shaped by the way society interacts with them, often in ways I don't experience at all. I find it fascinating, though I'm not sure I fully understand it.

'No, I just didn't think about them,' I continued. 'I think I came from a different generation, you know, the nineties, waif-thin, heroin-chic look. Nobody ever told me I was flat-chested, you know?'

'Nobody ever told you that you were flat-chested?' she repeated, as though she'd just dropped a bombshell. Her disbelief was genuine.

I took a deep breath, surprised that this was a point of contention. It suddenly occurred to me that she might have been seeing me through her lens – through the 'large breasts' lens. Could she have been unconsciously projecting that lens onto me? Had she seen me through the eyes of someone who felt that breasts – large, small, or somewhere in between – were an integral part of a woman's identity? In fact, that thought made me wonder how often we do that: assume that the physical shape of someone else's body is somehow tied to who they are as a person.

I continued, half-jokingly: 'Nope, never heard it.'

She looked at me, wide-eyed, as though the very concept was foreign to her. She looked down at her own chest, I'm guessing unconsciously, as if checking to make sure everything was still intact.

'Maybe behind my back,' I added with a wink. 'But genuinely, I've never heard it to my face.' I wanted to break the tension, to remind myself that this wasn't a topic of shame. We weren't talking about flat chests in a way that suggested there was something wrong with them.

'I'd never thought about getting a boob job until recently, probably because I'm exposed to all this boob-noise now,' my friend then said, sipping her wine with a knowing look.

At this point, I was fully immersed in the conversation, as I was becoming more aware of how much my friend had internalised the discourse around breasts. It was clear that her growing awareness of breast surgery wasn't just intellectual – it was emotional, too.

'Not to get them bigger, obviously,' she continued, seemingly undeterred by my blank look. 'But I figure after I have babies, they'll droop a lot, and I might have to get a mastopexy done.'

'Mastopexy?' I repeated. I wasn't even entirely sure how to spell it.

'You've never heard of a mastopexy?' she asked, incredulous. 'Wow. You really haven't thought much about breasts.' Her tone shifted to something approaching admiration mixed with disbelief.

'It's where they reshape the breast tissue and reposition the nipple,' she said, after a long pause.

'Oh, okay.' My confusion was palpable.

'You've never googled this stuff?' she asked, half-laughing but with genuine curiosity.

'No,' I replied. 'I've been exposed to all the breast stuff through the exploration of the book, but I've never personally googled procedures for myself. Have you?'

'All the time!' she replied, enthusiastically. 'Everyone does!'

'Everyone does?' I was struggling to catch up.

'Yes!' She wasn't backing down. 'Who's happy with their breasts? There's always something wrong with them.

One's bigger than the other, the nipples are unsightly, they droop, they're too big, they're too small. There's always something. I've been googling this kind of stuff since I was a teenager.'

'I didn't have the internet as a teenager,' I responded, offering a weak explanation for why I had clearly been living in some kind of ancient pre-Google era.

'That's right! I forgot how old you are!' she laughed, as if my age – my clearly ancient state – was some sort of relic I should be embarrassed about.

I rolled my eyes dramatically. Flat-chested and old, I thought. Honestly, if I had to take another one of these age-related jabs, I was going to have to start wearing a sign that said, 'Not Actually That Old!' But as we continued the conversation, I found myself oddly grateful for not having grown up in the age of relentless digital exposure and ubiquitous body-image standards.

In fact, every time I have a conversation about bodies and expectations, I am truly glad I grew up without the internet.

• • •

CHAPTER FORTY-THREE

The internet and breast anxiety

Since the advent of the internet, concerns and perceptions surrounding the appearance of breasts have undeniably evolved, influenced by various factors including media representation, social media and online communities. The internet has given us unprecedented access to a never-ending flood of information, images and discussions about body image. It's a bit like a global gossip session, only with a side of advertisements and algorithmic suggestions designed to remind you that your body doesn't quite measure up to whatever the 'ideal' is this week.

Let's talk about this new reality. One of the most prominent effects of the internet on perceptions of breast appearance is the rise of idealised standards. Oh yes, the internet has done its fair share of shaping the standard of beauty. Social media platforms, in particular, are like these glossy highlight reels where flawless bodies, especially breasts, are displayed like rare jewels in a museum. You know the ones – perfectly symmetrical, perky and not a single pore out of place. They belong to celebrities, influencers and models whose appearances seem to adhere to the unspoken rules of what we should all look like.

For those of us who don't see ourselves reflected in these pristine images, the internet can make it feel like we missed some critical memo on how to 'get it right'. It's like you're browsing a catalogue for an alternate universe in which everyone is taller and thinner, and, apparently, has been airbrushed into oblivion. This bombardment of 'perfect' images has created some rather unrealistic expectations for what constitutes attractive or desirable breasts, and – spoiler alert – they're often impossible to live up to.

But – and this is where it gets interesting – the internet hasn't just been about pushing these unreachable beauty standards. It has also created a space where people can share their personal stories, struggles and insecurities about body image, including breast appearance. Online forums, blogs and social media groups have become some of the most important platforms for people to talk openly about their bodies. It's like finding a hidden room full of strangers who, as it turns out, all share the same discomforts and doubts.

This online space has allowed individuals to find solace and camaraderie in knowing that concerns about breast appearance are not unique. You're not the only one who sometimes wonders why one breast is slightly bigger than the other or why your cleavage doesn't look like that of your favourite Instagram model. This virtual community of care offers validation, advice and the comforting realisation that, hey, we're all in this together.

If you thought you were the only one googling 'why are my breasts lopsided?', guess what? You're definitely not alone. And that's kind of comforting, right?

On the flip side, however, the internet has also normalised the idea of surgically altering breast appearance. The sheer volume of before-and-after photos floating around is utterly overwhelming. Breast augmentation, reduction and lifts are discussed so openly online, it's like flipping through a Rolodex of potential improvements. The normalisation of these procedures, complete with testimonials and results that look like they were engineered by a team of perfectionists, has subtly pushed the narrative that if your breasts don't look a certain way, maybe it's time to 'fix' them.

Here's the thing: cosmetic surgery isn't inherently bad, and if you choose that path, more power to you. But the sheer volume of images, endorsements and ads about 'perfect' breasts can sometimes make people feel like it's the only route to confidence. It's almost as if we've forgotten that breasts are, well, just a body part – there's no one-size-fits-all approach, and there's no rule book that says they have to be a specific shape or size to be 'right'. But the internet, ever the overachiever, continues to flood us with the idea that our natural, unaltered bodies might not be good enough as they are.

Amid all of this, however, there has been a refreshing shift. The internet has played a huge role in challenging the traditional standards of beauty, especially in relation to breasts. Online movements and campaigns advocating for body positivity have become louder and more visible.

Platforms are now filled with individuals celebrating diverse body shapes, sizes and, yes, breast shapes. People have started embracing natural variations in breast appearance, whether it's the shape, size or asymmetry. Suddenly, 'perfect' becomes whatever you feel good about.

But here's where things get a little messy: has it gone far enough? Sure, we've got movements pushing for diversity and inclusivity, and that's amazing. But we still consume digitally altered images at an unrelenting pace, and their sheer dominance still lingers in the back of our minds. There's still this nagging sense that there's a 'better' version of ourselves, somewhere, hiding beneath the natural. The pursuit of body positivity is undeniably important, but how much has it really shifted the dial on how we actually feel about ourselves? Are we really embracing all body types, or are we just trying to make ourselves feel better about not being able to compete with an Instagram influencer who's had more procedures than we've had avocado toast?

Let's not forget that the constant exposure to edited and filtered images on social media is contributing to a phenomenon called 'social comparison'. You've probably experienced it: you scroll through your feed, and all of a sudden, you're analysing your body like it's a Picasso painting that's gone horribly wrong. You compare your breasts to others' and, guess what? You don't measure up (at least in your mind). This can lead to feelings of inadequacy, self-doubt and dissatisfaction with your own body – feelings that are exacerbated by the unrealistic standards you're repeatedly shown. The issue isn't just that these images are edited; it's that we've started thinking they represent reality.

And then there's the other fun part of this digital age: cyberbullying and body shaming. Ah, yes, nothing quite says 'internet culture' like a comment section full of unsolicited opinions. If you thought the idea of people judging your appearance was bad enough in real life, brace yourself for the online critics. The internet has given rise to people who seem to believe it's their duty to tell you exactly how you should look – and if your breasts don't fit the mould, prepare for some harsh feedback. This digital scrutiny can have a lasting impact, making people feel self-conscious, anxious or even depressed. The internet's ability to magnify body-image concerns is something we can't ignore. After all, it's easier to send a cruel comment from behind a screen than to say it face to face, right?

So, what do we do with all of this? How do we manage this paradoxical relationship with the internet and our bodies, especially when it comes to something as personal as our breasts? The first step is recognising that the internet is not the ultimate arbiter of truth. Social media may present a curated version of reality, but it's not the only reality. Your body – your breasts – are yours. They don't need to meet anyone else's standards or expectations.

It's okay to appreciate what others choose to do with their bodies, but remember: no one's online persona is a reflection of the whole picture. People curate their lives to show what they want others to see, not necessarily the messy, imperfect and often humorous moments in between. So, when you're comparing your body to someone else's, keep that in mind. What you see online isn't the full story.

Ultimately, the internet has opened up a whole new world of possibilities for discussing body image and breast appearance. It's given us the opportunity to challenge outdated beauty norms and embrace a wider variety of body types. It's a space for support, for celebration and for sharing vulnerabilities. But, like everything in life, it requires balance. Embrace what makes you feel good, seek out spaces that celebrate real bodies and remember that perfection doesn't exist – not on the internet, not in magazines and certainly not in the mirror.

• • •

CHAPTER FORTY-FOUR

The leg woman

It was one of those afternoons where everything felt a bit ... chaotic. The trampoline party had just wrapped up, and I was still feeling the effects of the madness – sore legs, a throbbing headache from all the high-pitched kid screams, and the vague feeling that I'd somehow ended up in an alternate universe where children had more energy than the entire population of a small country.

I wiped the sweat off my forehead and collapsed into a chair next to Ita, who was also looking a little worse for wear. She'd been over in the corner, clapping enthusiastically as our daughters launched themselves into the air, each girl determined to defy gravity, if only for a moment.

'I simply don't understand where they get this kind of energy from,' I said, slumping down and looking at my legs in sheer disbelief.

'I think they're fuelled by pure chaos and sugar,' Ita replied, laughing. 'I haven't even gotten on a trampoline, and my calves feel like they're about to explode.'

'Well, I'm definitely not going near one of those things again without a few weeks of training. My legs are jelly right now.'

We both stared at the girls, who were bouncing in unison as if they were a synchronised trampoline team. I wasn't sure how they managed to stay so light and carefree while I felt like an overcooked noodle. I could almost hear my knees creaking in protest.

'Do you think they'll remember this as one of those iconic childhood moments?' Ita asked, tilting her head toward the chaos. 'You know, the trampoline phase. Or will they look back and be all, "Ugh, why were we so obsessed with jumping up and down in a confined space?"'

'Definitely the latter,' I said, sipping my water. 'The second they hit puberty, it's all going to be about the clothes, the crop tops and *not* wanting to be seen bouncing around in public like a human pogo stick.'

Ita nodded sagely. 'Oh god. Don't remind me. My daughter's already at the age where she's experimenting with *fashion choices* that are ... well, let's just say I'm not ready for crop tops to be her new normal.'

I chuckled. 'Tell me about it. My daughter's in this weird phase where she's noticing things about her body for the first time, and she's so confused'.

'Same!' Ita laughed. 'One minute, she's proudly declaring she wants to wear a crop top, and the next minute, she's asking, "Do I look like I'm trying too hard?" and I'm like, "Honey, you're *twelve*. No one expects you to have it all figured out."'

I couldn't help but laugh. It was such a classic pre-teen thing to do. They're at that age where they're *so* close to figuring themselves out, but it's just awkward enough to make everything feel like an existential crisis.

'And don't even get me started on the *boob talk*,' I added, trying to sound nonchalant, but secretly feeling like I'd just opened Pandora's box. 'My daughter's not quite there yet, but I can see it coming. She hasn't started asking questions, but you know it's only a matter of time.'

Ita's eyes widened, and she leaned in. 'Oh, the boob talk. I'm bracing myself for that moment with my daughter. She's already googling "Why do women have boobs?" and "What are boobs supposed to do?" and I'm over here like, "Please, just let me have five minutes of peace before we dive into that discussion."'

I nodded sympathetically. 'It's insane. I didn't even *think* about my boobs until I was thirty-eight. I was just like, "Oh yeah, those are there. Cool. Whatever." I swear, my boobs had no real impact on my life. I went about my day, lived my life and I never really had any major concerns about them. And then, all of a sudden, I'm in my late thirties and ... *bam*. The whole world wants to talk about them.'

Ita stared at me in disbelief. 'Wait. You're telling me that for thirty-eight years, you didn't think about your boobs? At all?'

'Not once,' I said, shrugging. 'I mean, sure, I'd notice them occasionally – when I went bra shopping, or when I tried on a shirt that didn't fit quite right. But they weren't on my mind. I didn't obsess over them. I wasn't one of those people who was always like, "Oh, my boobs are too small" or "Oh, my boobs are too big." I just ... didn't care.'

Ita's mouth dropped open. 'That's incredible. *No way*. I mean, but clearly, you're a leg woman.'

'A *what* woman?'

'You know. A *leg* woman,' she repeated. 'You're not a boob person. You've got fantastic legs. Not boobs. You're just ... I don't know. A leg woman.'

I blinked at her, trying to process what she'd just said. 'I'm a leg woman? Is that a real thing?'

Ita nodded enthusiastically. 'Men are divided into a series of camps. The boob camp, the leg camp and the general idiot camp. There's crossover in the mix too.'

I stared at her in disbelief. 'Wait, you're telling me there are people who ... like legs more than boobs?'

'Yep,' she said, nodding with the kind of serious confidence you only see in people who are fully convinced they've stumbled upon some hidden truth about the universe. 'It's a real category, and I think you fit it. You're a leg woman.'

'Well, that's the most ridiculous thing I've ever heard,' I said, bursting into laughter.

Ita grinned. 'We all have our preferences. Some people are boob people. Some people are leg people. And some people – well, some people are just furry animals or something, like the furries.'

'I don't think that's quite what furries are about ...' I mumble.

'You know what I mean. Don't overcomplicate it. You're a leg woman.'

'I'm a leg woman,' I repeated, like it was some sort of yogic mantra.

'You're a leg woman,' she said, with a rapid nod of the head.

• • •

CHAPTER FORTY-FIVE

Body dysmorphic disorder

Thinking about the conversations I was having with friends, I started reading journal articles on body dysmorphic disorder, particularly in relation to boobs. Colloquially, body dysmorphic disorder (BDD) can be described as a mental health condition where a person becomes excessively preoccupied with perceived flaws or defects in their appearance. These flaws may be minor or even imagined, but they cause significant distress and can lead to obsessive thoughts and compulsive behaviours, and can impair a person's daily functioning.

People with BDD often spend a lot of time scrutinising their appearance in mirrors – or they avoid mirrors altogether. They may seek reassurance from others about their appearance or engage in repetitive behaviours like grooming, checking or comparing themselves with others. Despite others' reassurances, individuals with BDD remain convinced that their perceived flaws make them unattractive or abnormal.

This disorder can affect any part of the body, but common areas of concern include skin, hair, nose, eyes, breasts, and overall body shape or size. The preoccupation with these perceived flaws can lead to feelings of shame, anxiety and depression, impacting relationships, work and overall quality of life.

I read about a young woman who has been binding her breasts since she was 12 years old because she believes them to be too big. She spent hours in front of the mirror each day assessing her breasts. She had anxiety and depression, and even suicidal thoughts. She didn't express any gender concerns – she believed herself to be a girl – but her boobs came to occupy her thoughts completely.

At a later age, she decided to have a double mastectomy, removing her breasts altogether.

The journal articles make me incredibly sad. They meticulously outline each person's mental, social and familial backgrounds. Even though the majority of people have an underlying condition – obsessive-compulsive disorder, borderline personality disorder and so on – I find myself wondering how this world has contributed to this fixation. These feelings of inadequacy, of worthlessness? This single-minded focus on a body part that doesn't really look the same for any of us?

I start thinking about my own children, and whether they'll be made to feel inadequate. Maybe they already do.

It's so strange, because they are all so incredibly beautiful and perfect.

• • •

CHAPTER FORTY-SIX

Free the nipple! Or, at least, the obsession with it

Amanda

You didn't think I would just leave it there, did you? After all that hoo-ha about wanting smaller boobs and hating my body? Surely you'd want to know what happened next. Was I finally happy? Did I become dateable and meet someone and settle down, all because my boobs were a third smaller than they had been?

Well, now I can tell you: it wasn't that dramatic.

The first few weeks after the surgery, I was pissed off. I thought I'd gone 'too small', even though my boobs were still 'huge', according to my friends.

By a few days post-surgery, I had decided I was going to have them made bigger again. I'd made a mistake and missed my old boobs, I decided. And, once again, the intense feelings of discontentment swirled around.

Then, when all the drugs wore off, and I settled

back into the Pilates studio and into the gym, wearing my old clothes (which were now more flattering) and realising I could still fit into my usual bras (just a little more comfortably), I didn't even think about my boobs. I really didn't.

It was weird. It was as if I was ... happy? A feeling I hadn't felt in a while.

What about the men? The attention? The validation? And the women? How was the judgement? The stares? The sniggers?

I put my profile on a dating app – non-booby photos – and started going on dates as practice. I wore gym gear and tight tops and no one really stared at my boobs. Women didn't look, men didn't follow me, and you know what? I barely even noticed.

I've had a few flings, had a few boyfriends. Not one of them mentioned the size of my breasts. Not a single one. I didn't even think about it.

Not once have I lamented the loss of my enormous 1050cc breasts. I tried life with 'the best in Australia!', and it didn't bring me much happiness – for a myriad of complex reasons that I have tried to explain.

Now, a year on from the surgery, when I look in the mirror, I like my body. Sure, my boobs are still big, but they're not 'in your face', so to speak. They just fit nicely. I don't feel self-conscious the minute I walk out the door.

Some days I miss the attention, but mostly I am very

happy with my new look. My friends think it's hilarious. 'You've still got massive boobs,' says my best friend Tab, rolling her eyes, on the odd day that I reminisce about my old boobs with rose-tinted spectacles.

But clothes fit and look better and my new body reflects the autumnal years of my life. (I'm not in God's waiting room yet but I bloody feel like it sometimes. Thank god for HRT.)

My boobs no longer define me. But it wasn't so much the work I've had done to my body that has shaped that. It has been the work I've done inside.

I worked out that validation from men didn't really make me happy. Sure, it was an ego boost, but it wasn't real. Men weren't interested in *me*, Amanda. They wanted to see my tits. Not all of them, but enough of them for me to feel shit about myself, because I worried if they knew the real me, they wouldn't be interested.

I do still care what people think, despite my public bravado. I would love to say that no woman cares what men think, that those days are gone. It's just not true for all of us, is it? Still, there's a subtle shift happening in my fifties. I care, sure, but I care less. I've swapped the tight-fitting tops from Kookai ('the hooker's uniform', those in the industry used to joke) for crisp, classy white shirts. I've realised 'sensual and sophisticated' is just as sexy, if not more, than wearing tops that skim past the nipple. Now I am dressing for me. And I really like the way I look.

Since retiring from life as Samantha X, I've had to strip my skin. Literally. I've worked out real beauty isn't about the biggest boobs or the blondest hair.

It comes from within. And if you're reading this, wishing you were bigger, smaller, thinner, curvier, bigger bum, smaller bum – STOP. Don't waste your energy and your life wishing you were different, and imagining that your life would just be perfect if you had a different body.

It wouldn't be. Your life won't magically be perfect if your boobs are bigger. You'll just have bigger boobs.

You are perfect the way you are.

(PS: You didn't think I'd leave you wondering what the secret to good skin was, did you? It's ... wait. Maybe there's another book in that.)

• • •

CHAPTER FORTY-SEVEN

Breast decisions

In July of my 42nd year, I make an unconventional decision: I decide not to get my boobs done. Around the same time, I make another rebellious choice: I won't get married again. These two decisions, in their own way, are tied together with the loose thread of rebellion that's been running through my life like an undercurrent, never fully visible but always there.

Let's start with the boobs. It's a subject that's been popping up more often than I'd care to admit – like an unexpected guest at a dinner party who keeps finding their way into the conversation – and obviously, it's also a result of the book.

When a friend recently asked, 'So, when are you going to get your boobs done?', I laughed it off. But the truth is, I've never really been tempted by the idea of implants. The decision not to get them was never a big 'Aha!' moment. It was more of a gradual realisation that I didn't need to change a thing about my body to feel good about myself.

It's hard to pinpoint the moment when I became so comfortable with my flat-chested self, but I'll say this: it probably wasn't when I was growing up. Back then, there was no Instagram, no TikTok and no curated beauty standards that told me what I should look like. I was skinny enough to be thought of as 'cool' without any boobs, and no one ever called me 'flat-chested' or made me feel inadequate. In fact, the absence of breasts was never a topic for discussion – mainly because nobody seemed to care. And I mean, really, why should they? But let's be real – there were always curated beauty standards, only they were in the form of magazines and movies and Hollywood stars and models: they were the ones that told me I should be skinny. Always.

Flash-forward a couple of decades. I'm sitting in a coffee shop with an old colleague of mine drinking frothy cappuccinos. She's 27, and she and her boyfriend have decided to get married. 'Look at this one,' she says, showing me a photo of a diamond ring. 'It's an emerald cut. Isn't it stunning?' I stare at the photo, vaguely aware that the diamond is, indeed, shiny, but with no clue what an 'emerald cut' actually is. My friend, a true connoisseur of all things bridal, excitedly points out that this particular cut is 'elegant' and 'classic'.

I nod along, trying to hide my absolute confusion. What happened to just 'diamond-shaped'? But she's undeterred, showing me more and more pictures of diamonds with names of cuts I've never heard of – cushion, oval, round. 'I think I like the oval one,' she says, scrolling through her endless list of options.

As if the diamond drama weren't enough, she then tells me she's had her acrylic stiletto nails removed. 'I need to grow out my natural nails for the proposal,' she says, her eyes wide with excitement. 'You know, for the photos. I don't want whorish nails when he proposes – something more feminine, like Funny Bunny nails.' At this point, I'm doing my best not to laugh out loud because, honestly, I have no idea what 'whorish nails' are, nor do I understand why this moment has to be so meticulously curated. But I keep my poker face on because I don't want to reveal my utter ignorance about both diamonds and nails. Maybe I'm just a geek, as someone pointed out to me recently.

But as I sip my coffee and nod in understanding (well, I'm pretending to understand), I'm reminded of something: I don't get this. The whole wedding thing, the ring thing, the nails thing – it all feels a little too 'on brand' for something I'm just not interested in. I'm a little too old, a little too self-aware and a lot too comfortable in my own skin to care much about things like emerald cuts and Funny Bunny nails.

That's not to say I don't love my friend – I do, deeply. I'm genuinely happy for her and her excitement about the proposal and the future she's building. But somewhere in the back of my mind, a tiny voice whispers, 'Is this what I'm supposed to want?'

The answer is clear: no, I don't think it is. I've made my peace with the idea that I don't need a ring to validate my relationships, and I don't need implants to feel attractive.

That's when I think of Antigone – yes, the Greek heroine. Antigone was a woman who knew her essence wasn't defined by external appearances. Whether she had big boobs, small boobs or no boobs at all didn't matter. What mattered was her will, her principles and her determination. It was her inner strength, her defiance of the state's authority, that defined her. She taught me that being true to yourself is the ultimate act of rebellion. And if that means rocking a flat chest for the rest of my life, then so be it.

I think about Connor, who taught me that there's no one right way to do gender. Gender isn't about conforming to a mould, and it certainly isn't about meeting some arbitrary standard of attractiveness. It's about expressing yourself authentically, regardless of whether or not society approves.

Amanda, too, has been a guiding force in my life. Her clever, no-nonsense approach to everything from relationships to self-image reminded me that we don't always find who we are easily. Sometimes, it takes a journey. But that journey – whether it involves wedding rings, breast augmentation or anything else – should be uniquely ours. It's not for anyone else to decide.

And so, I decided that my final act of rebellion would be to leave my body exactly as it is. It's not a bold declaration to the world – it's just me, accepting the fact that my body, in all its post-forties glory, is good enough. Breasts or no breasts, wrinkles or no wrinkles, my body is my body, and I'm done with the notion that it needs to be fixed, adjusted or augmented to be worthy.

Let's be clear: I'm not anti-boobs. Hell, I'm all for augmented breasts on other women. We all have the right to do what makes us feel empowered and comfortable in our own skin. And if that means getting a boob job, getting a tattoo or getting a diamond ring to announce to the world that we're in a committed relationship, more power to us.

But what's equally important is that we normalise the conversation around body image, around what it means to be a woman, and around the unspoken expectations that often leave people feeling inadequate or worthless. It's time to be open about bodies, imperfections and choices.

But let's not pretend it's easy. It's hard not to feel the pressure of a world that seems obsessed with the appearance of our bodies, with labels like 'perfect' and 'imperfect', with expectations of what a woman's body should look like at every stage of her life. And yet, the most radical thing I can do is reject all of it. I don't need a diamond ring to validate my relationship, and I don't need bigger breasts to feel attractive. I just need to be me.

That said, I'm not ruling out the possibility of changing my mind in the future. I reserve the right to get implants, get married again or do whatever the hell I feel like doing. But for now, I'll continue to rock my flat chest and embrace the rebellion of just being myself. Because, in the end, isn't that what we're all really looking for? Authenticity? Freedom to be who we are, without apology?

Here's to owning our bodies, our choices and our journeys – whether they include diamonds, implants or none of the above. Let's keep the conversation going. Let's make it fun, let's make it honest and, above all, let's make it *ours*.

• • •

CHAPTER FORTY-EIGHT

A letter to our daughters

To our daughters,

As you grow and begin to experience the changes that come with becoming a woman, we want to take a moment to talk to you about something that may feel confusing, awkward or even uncomfortable at times: your breasts.

In a world that often associates women's bodies with judgement or expectation, we want to remind you that your body is yours, and it is incredible. What you're going through is something that has evolved for millions of years, and while we don't have all the answers to why certain things happen, there is beauty in the way your body changes and adapts, just as there has been beauty in every human who has lived before you.

Breasts are a symbol of femininity in many cultures, but they are also so much more than that. Your breasts are part of you, just as your hands, feet and heart are. They are tools and symbols, and above all they are reminders of your power and your identity as a woman in a world that is constantly evolving.

When you're older and possibly become mothers, you'll learn that breasts also serve a life-giving role. They nourish and sustain. The way you're able to provide for a baby by breastfeeding is a miraculous gift. Breasts have evolved to ensure that babies can feed safely and comfortably, without risk of suffocation. This beautiful part of your body is essential to the cycle of life. But remember that this nurturing ability is just one part of the multifaceted beauty of your body.

For now, it's important to know that as your body changes, it's just one phase of your amazing, lifelong journey. Your breasts will change in size and shape, and that's okay. Some days they might feel awkward. Some days they might feel empowering. You may love them, you may feel uncertain about them – it's all valid. Your feelings about your body, including your breasts, will ebb and flow, and that's totally natural. What's important is that you feel empowered in your choices. Whether you choose to embrace them, modify them or just let them be, remember that every change is a sign of your body's power and resilience.

As you enter a phase of life that will likely bring you into contact with messages about how women 'should' look or behave, know that these messages often don't reflect the diversity and beauty of women's bodies. There is no one-size-fits-all when it comes to breasts or body shape. Society might try to tell you how breasts should look, how big they should be or how they should feel, but remember: your body is yours, and it is unique to you.

In a world full of images that might make you feel like you have to live up to a certain standard, we want to remind you that the most important thing is your health and wellbeing. You are beautiful as you are. Your body, as it changes, is a beautiful expression of the person you are becoming. Breasts are just one part of that journey – and there's so much more to who you are than the way your body looks.

We also encourage you to show compassion to other women. Each of us has our own journey with our bodies, and some of us may feel more confident than others; some of us may love our breasts, and others may not. We want you to support each other through the ups and downs, and to always remember that no one else gets to dictate how you should feel about yourself. We all deserve respect, understanding and kindness.

As you look to the future, we want you to always remember that your breasts, and your body as a whole, will change over time. What feels new and unfamiliar now will one day be something you'll look back on with wisdom and understanding. Every wrinkle, every curve, every stretch mark is a story – a chapter in your life that marks growth, strength and resilience. And those changes? They don't define you; they are part of the incredible journey of life.

When you're older, you might one day share the same wisdom with your own daughters. You'll have the chance to pass down the same love and support you're receiving now. Just as we want to offer you a message of love and compassion, we hope you'll give that same support to the next generation, teaching them that bodies are beautiful in all their forms.

In the meantime, know that we're here for you, ready to listen, to laugh, to cry and to support you through every stage of your journey. You are perfect as you are, and we will always be proud of the women you are becoming.

With all our love,

Lisa and Amanda

• • •

Acknowledgements

We would like to acknowledge some very special people who helped bring this book to life.

To Diana and Juliet, and the entire team at Echo Publishing, thank you for believing in our vision for *Boobs*, a curious and unconventional little book. Your sensitivity, insight and editorial brilliance brought a depth and nuance to this work that few could match.

To our editors, the designer of our beautiful cover, and everyone behind the scenes who made this book a reality, thank you for your skill, care and commitment.

To the people who generously shared their stories: Antigone, Susan and Connor, your bravery and truth-telling moved us deeply. To Libby, thank you for planting the seed of the 'boob-droopage-while reading' idea. And to Dr Moradi, thank you for sharing your knowledge and insight with such generosity and thoughtfulness.

To our families, friends and loved ones, thank you for your unwavering support, humour and love. This book wouldn't exist without you.